AF364916

1st edition

ISBN:
978-87-974548-2-4 (paperback)
978-87-974548-3-1 (hardback)
978-87-974548-4-8 (ebook)
978-87-974548-5-5 (audio)
978-87-974548-6-2 (dbk)

Author: Gitte Madelaire
Book coach: Malene Bendtsen
Proofreading: Kathrine Krake
Cover and layout: Diren Yardimli
Illustrations: Tine Faurby Stilborg

 www.energeticleadership.eu

For complementary material, please visit www.energeticleadership.eu/resources

Energetic Leadership

GITTE MADELAIRE

Contents

CONTENTS

Foreword

Employees and managers yearn for meaning in their work. They are fed up with tasks and corporate purposes that don't align with their vision for the world, diminishing the effects of common leadership practices.

What if the people in your organisation also no longer want to work simply to get a salary? What if they, like many others, want to enjoy retirement in their 40s and 90s – joining the rising age rebellion that could make the last phase of life the coolest phase of all?

What if your employees and managers are only just perched on their office chairs, clocked out mentally, and spend their weekends thinking about other options? And put into a larger perspective, what if the rebellion against meaninglessness is a general phenomenon – spreading at lightning speed like a ripple effect – and a fundamental change in what working life is about is to hit every organisation?

What if the future belongs to the individual, and the energy rooted in your employees' and customers' burning desire to make the world a better place and save the planet and its inhabitants is the very foundation for building your organisation's sense of the future? What if, in reality, the pressure from the bottom of your organisation is exactly what you need to make more money and be much stronger in the future?

Welcome to reality. We're facing the most significant change in what business and leadership are all about since the invention of the assembly line. Yesterday's management regime is no good if we are to develop stable organisations that can deliver on the world's demands for sustainability, both internally and externally. The air has gone out of the balloon. Half the workforce is simply ditching jobs to find more meaningful workplaces. The other half is either working themselves to pieces, turning up without bringing their souls and basically couldn't care less, or driven primarily by fear.

While that's putting it bluntly, there is hope if leaders dare to lean into the underlying spiritual and planetary movement that is increasingly permeating our society. What is happening is a true paradigm shift and an emerging rebellion that should not be underestimated in a leadership context. We demand a new kind of leadership and community that aims to heal the planet and create healthy and meaningful work lives.

From quantum physics, we know that everything in the universe consists of energy and relationships. Interestingly, these are also the two tools used in management to make decisions and evoke motivation. In other words, we depend on producing vibrant and sufficient energy and connecting in communities.

A majority of people living on planet Earth believe that there is "something" out there that is more extensive than themselves. Maybe you're religious and use prayer to form an energetic relationship; maybe you're more spiritual and use manifestation; or maybe you're more in the corporate camp that focuses on motivation and culture, on having ambition and vision, imagination, and curiosity.

It's quite interesting that people worldwide increasingly believe that there is something more, bigger and different between us that we can't see. That there is an energy and relationship outside of us that we can access. If we want better well-being, a better economy, a beautiful society, and better use of our resources, we must dare to transform ourselves and each other and tap into that energy.

We may each call the energetic force something different. What is certain is that if you know how to use it as a leader, you are well prepared for the future.

Anne Skare Nielsen
Chief futurist, Universal Futurist

*To all the everyday heroes out there who,
through your leadership, seek to shape the world we are all a part of.*

*This book is written to help you succeed in bringing out the true potential in
yourself and your organisation so you can stand strong in a changing world
and create our shared future.*

To my family.

René – my loving, patient husband.

*Martin, Morten, and Michael – my wise sons, children of the new age,
who show me the future every day.*

*Thank you to everyone in my family, all friends and "colleagues"
in my futurist universe and network in general
who have helped make this book a reality.*

I am deeply grateful to all of you.

Introduction

A changing world

Never before have we faced so many global crises directly impacting our lives and businesses. We are simultaneously experiencing geo-political, macroeconomic, microeconomic, climate, biodiversity, and resource crises, all impacting companies' value chains and markets – as well as our personal finances, security, and sense of fulfilment.

In this situation, it's easy to overlook the organisational and human crises that are unfolding right now in the vast majority of companies, which are crucial to their survival and ability to co-create the transformations the world needs. Discontent has never been more prevalent, and employee loyalty and engagement have never been lower. And that's mainly because the way we manage ourselves has changed significantly. We're not content with the same as yesterday, and yesterday's leadership is no longer sufficient.

We need to develop a stronger capacity for forward-thinking and a new approach to leadership that fits the world we are and will increasingly be a part of as businesses are facing two main challenges:

1. Customer, government and employee demands for circular sustainability models and regenerative strategies to solve global challenges require leadership with cohesion and meaning.
2. The most important competitive parameter of the future – and thus competence – is the mastery of energetic language, intuition and the ability to create coherence between the purpose of employees' personal lives and the purpose of the organisation.

Both of these challenges are rarely well supported by the often fragmented projects/programmes at the heart of many companies' operations. They require a form of leadership far from current practices, with a much greater focus on purpose and meaning for the individual, on tapping into and creating energy, and on developing a stronger sense of the future. I call it "future-sense".

Future-sense is generally perceived as the ability to innovate, discover or create new needs in the market. In that context, future-sense is defined solely as an analytical and rational ability to develop and execute good ideas. It easily becomes about technology leaps, new partnerships, and mergers.

Such a definition has proven to be inadequate because even though we've spent decades developing new ways to innovate, have plenty of new project management systems, lots of data, and have invented agile development methods, absenteeism is still rising, employee and customer loyalty is plummeting, and the planet is suffering.

There is room for improvement. We all know that. But many people don't yet realise the slowly developing underlying change in the mentality of customers and the organisation. As an extension of this, there needs to be more attention paid to the real driving force behind the challenges; a pronounced degree of decoupling of the commercial sense and the human energetic sense.

For centuries, humans in the workplace have been a resource whose capacity has often been measured in hours. We haven't paid enough attention to the fact that the quality of time depends on our ability to fulfil deep inner needs – and we haven't created the conditions to keep employees not only happy but to keep them healthy and activate the true potential of each individual and the community.

We, as humans, are connected in an energy web (which quantum physics can now also measure). But over time, we have forgotten our first language, the language of energy. In a materially focused and scientifically driven age, we have forgotten to listen inwards, to be patient and to practise the gift of connecting our energetic sense and our rational commercial sense. We must relearn this connection because it can give us the courage and energy to dare to fulfil our potential as humans and organisations. We must lean on intuitive foresight and rebuild our energetic sense of the future. For a better world. For better health. And for a better life.

Crises and new technology have fueled the fear of layoffs and personal financial problems – no doubt about it. But there's also no doubt that managers and employees have significantly changed not only their behaviour but also their values and mindset about the role of work and the workplace in their lives. Demands for meaningful work are no longer negotiable, and the new generations' heightened sense of human potential (and the planet's problems) is increasingly influencing leadership – but often invisibly and without recognition or articulation.

This book helps to create a new awareness of what it means to be a leader and what it means to be human, shedding light on the often overlooked factors that are paramount to business success. These factors have always been present, but the need to recognise them has been strongly reinforced by several societal trends that can no longer be ignored in leadership and have the power to determine who and which organisations will survive and thrive in the new world.

The change in our inner and outer worlds, which is currently in full swing, will very soon openly demand action. The kind of management – of ourselves, our companies, and our society – which has led us to where we are today cannot counteract the problems the world is facing. It also falls short of attracting and retaining healthy and engaged employees.

Future-sense in modern leadership – which is not like yesterday's – is about (re)connecting the commercial sense and the energetic sense so that we can evoke and activate the true potential of leaders, employees, organisations, and markets. It is the energetic sense of progress that ensures healthy businesses that know how to deliver on all dimensions: to make good money, to provide health, jobs and job satisfaction, to be a positive and integral part of nature and its resources, and to contribute positively to humanity through the values it practises.

For the first time, perhaps ever, the skills we need are not a question of new fads, new professional disciplines, new technology or any of the other tools we are accustomed to relying on. What is unique about the reality we are in now is that it requires us to rethink and redevelop what leadership and well-being competencies are.

Energetic sense of the future

If we are to avoid losing control of ourselves and the organisation in an unstable and changing world, that also affects our inner lives on an individual level. We must create a new beginning and reboot our leadership skills.

The last few years have clearly shown that we cannot control the conditions we work and live in. In other words, we urgently need a new model for education and learning that fits the future society and our perception of the human role in it.

In contrast to the prevailing practice, the leadership model proposed in this book is not only based on our brains but also rooted in our hearts and souls. The most crucial element in developing resilience, intuitive foresight and innovation is the individual's own energetic leadership: the ability to have conscious and deep contact with oneself, the ability to create oneself from within rather than adapting to external conditions that are in disharmony with the inner self, and the ability to evoke and make room for the same in others.

The oscillations in the heart's magnetic field are 5,000 times more potent than the oscillations of the brain[1], and when we lead with our intuition, our clarity amplifies. There's a reason we feel the urge to "follow our heart", but it's remarkable that we've created a culture where the brain is the boss and analytical approaches are required for most things – especially decision-making.

In the book mBraining by Grant Soosalu and Marvin Oka, the authors explain that we can use intuition to tune into the energies of others and go far beyond empathy, as we intuitively sense the unspoken and unconscious across time and space. That's why intuition is essential to leadership – but we've forgotten how to use it – and even often shamed intuition and failed to recognise it as a valid basis for decision-making. "Following your heart" doesn't belong in the workplace.

But if the people steering the ship ashore are not in touch with the horizon, their inner self, and how the crew and guests on board are feeling, then the ship is sailing without a rudder, and there's little chance of a consensus on the direction in which to steer it.

This is true even if everyone outwardly says the same thing because we all have our own personal calling, cause, or journey – and where we used to accept the discrepancy between our inner self and our day-to-day activities on the job, we now desert and find a better ship to muster, build a better ship, or even call for mutiny. We no longer want to live in disharmony with our inner self. That's what's new!

Business is sleepwalking into an era of conscious quitting.

Paul Polman[2]

It destroys our engagement, health, and sense of self when we feel forced to ignore our increasingly loud inner voice. Resigning ourselves to leaving our soul and personality at home when we go to work. We all want to be seen, heard, met and understood first and foremost. And we especially want to be heard, seen and respected by ourselves.

A common misconception is that this needs to be solved by developing the courage in employees to raise their hands and be honest, or to be insistent (and annoying) and persistently shout louder when the ship is heading to Bananas, not the Bahamas, and no one hears the call.

There is no need to shout louder. Instead, we need to leave yesterday's leadership behind and believe in ourselves enough to dare unleash the true potential of the company's leaders and employees. To contribute at our full capacity and not just the part perceived as welcome.

It is the courage to listen, both to others and especially to our inner self, we need to develop so that what we say and do is not detached from our soul. We need to relearn how to connect with ourselves and each other. Because when we are in better inner balance as human beings, we also create better outer balance.

These skills are necessary not only for organisations but also for individuals. They are also necessary to recreate the entire society sustainably. How we go to school, how we educate ourselves, our healthcare system, how we take care of children and older people, how we protect nature, what we produce or don't produce more of, how we create partnerships and communities with others locally, nationally and globally, and how we define welfare and the foundation that supports it. It's the entire structure of society that we need to look at.

We are thoroughly done with leadership built on fear. Fear of speaking up, of listening to our inner self, of losing our job, our salary, our home, and, in turn, our status and the respect of those around us. We're also done with fear's cousins: darkness, missed opportunities and dreams, and blocked energy.

We need a new beginning where leadership is trust, light, and abundant free-flowing energy. We need to rediscover what we already know in our heads but haven't allowed to enter our leadership practice in any significant form.

The Energetic Leadership Model presented in this book is my invention and inspired by two things:

1. Everything is energy, and there is an infinite amount of energy in the universe available to humans
2. The notion of being able to collect all information and analyse it to find truth is wrong. Our external and internal worlds are constantly changing. The potential of leadership and the opportunity to positively impact the world are, therefore, infinite.

The Energetic Leadership Model can be applied by all leaders, and for that matter, by all people, because we are all leaders in our own lives. The new true leadership is infinite when body, mind and soul are one in their communication – both in personal and corporate leadership.

This book is primarily for modern business leaders and emphasises openness, community, and growing together as individuals and organisations. As a leader, you must walk the walk and learn the skill yourself before passing it on.

For this reason, there is a need to work with the reconnection of the commercial sense and the energetic leadership on three levels:

- How the company can *develop* future-sense and Energetic Leadership as competence and make it part of the company's culture and management style
- How you, on a *personal* level, practise self-leadership and lead in harmony with your inner self
- How to train and practise that competence in your leadership of others

Developing the skills to feel deeply, listen attentively, observe keenly, and believe wholeheartedly is paramount to your personal and professional growth. It is the foundation of future-sense and gives you a sense of where you are and where your heart and soul want to go. You might think that to feel, listen, and see is something you already know, and faith has something to do with religion. But I promise you that if you follow the book's recommendations, you'll find that these skills develop exponentially and that you may have had the abilities, but the potential for using them has not been realised at all.

This book is, first and foremost, an inspiration and training book, full of exercises and questions that are manageable but sometimes difficult to answer. You can try out the things that come most naturally to you first. Take note of what makes you turn to a particular section. It could also indicate what's pulling you from within that needs attention. In other words, where is your energy guiding you?

I hope you revisit the book later. Once you've started exercising, you'll also read it with new eyes.

Happy reading!
GITTE MADELAIRE

About this book

This book consists of eight main chapters. You can dive into the last five as needed, but the first three chapters require a little more focus before moving on.

Chapter 1 explains the Energetic Leadership Model and how to use it to develop novel skills and capacity for change as an individual, in a leadership role, and as a company.

Chapter 2 reviews nine societal trends often ignored in leadership work and rapidly undermining yesterday's leadership styles.

Chapter 3 focuses on how humans function, including the energetic force, and why a future mindset is rooted precisely there. We also look at the connection between energetic factors, physiological factors, intelligence, and healthy and harmonious creativity.

Chapter 4 addresses the fact that when we start to take a closer look at the meeting between the two dimensions of the Energetic Leadership Model, it quickly gives rise to adjusting management practices in basic operations. Instead of providing general instructions, the book enters the concrete world, i.e. the various vital functions and tasks that must be solved in the organisation's operations. Because even though the methodology recommended is fairly universal, the realities to which it is applied differ, and the conditions that need to be revisited are, therefore, not the same either.

Chapter 5 on constructive behaviours gets to grips with the new methods and routines that can bring management into the future and develop a sense of the future on a daily basis.

Chapter 6 deals with developing the organisation's relevance, core delivery, communication of this, and the ability to execute and create momentum.

Chapters 7 and 8 guide you through how to evoke the full potential in the individual, the organisation, and the bottom line in a sustainable and growth-oriented way when future-sense is fuelled by energetic awareness.

At the end of the book, you will find cases that illustrate how you, as a leader, can mature and develop when you bring your curiosity and reflective sense of the future into play. The book is based on a number of interviews with leaders who have experienced the problems that arise when the energetic perspective is ignored.

Finally, at the back of the book, you will find an overview of the 11 exercises recommended in the book, as well as a glossary.

Energetic Leadership

Energy from a historical perspective

Our forefathers and foremothers were much better at appreciating and cultivating the gift of being with our soul and heart, at one with nature. But most of us, in our pursuit of provable knowledge, have forgotten to honour the wisdom and the ability to know that we are born with.

The intuitive mind is the sacred gift and the rational mind is the faithful servant. We have created a society that honors the servant and has forgotten the gift.

- Einstein

Ahead of his time, or perhaps even in tune with his time, Einstein describes the situation in the world, in organisations and people quite effectively. The ugly truth boiled down to a Maggi cube: We have problems, and we have created them ourselves.

Einstein has also already given us the solution: go back to honouring intuition as "the sacred gift". In another of his other famous quotes, he warns against falling back into the familiar:

We cannot solve our problems with the same thinking we used when we created them

- Einstein

To find new solutions to our challenges, we need to develop a different mindset (consciousness). That's the core of what I'm trying to get to in this book. How do we find our gifts so that we can solve the challenges we face?

We humans are extremely good at adapting and evolving. We have reinvented ourselves many times before. We've researched, developed and acquired new knowledge. But this century is different – not just because we need to acquire knowledge faster than ever. We now need to obtain the skills to rediscover and apply a whole new kind of knowledge, the knowledge we already contain, which cannot be scientifically proven but requires faith and trust in our senses.

The new thing we need to learn or relearn is to use our entire body, mind and soul to lead from a place where the three are one. Over the last many centuries, we have lost the connection between the three, leading as if from a one-legged chair or as the "driver" of a unicycle. It's possible, but it's exhausting, and it's hardly the fastest way to get where we want to go. It's not always pretty, either.

But what exactly is it that we have forgotten?

Simply put, since the discovery of quantum physics, we have known that everything is made up of energy and has an energy field. We humans are also an energy field. Raising awareness is always a journey of maturation, and it has indeed taken time for us to realise that we are energy – to become aware of it. Most of all, we are probably more ready for the realisation now because we have concrete evidence for the claim through measurements from the world of physics. But there is sometimes a long way to go from having the knowledge and being aware to knowing what to do with it.

It's old news, really, because many of our forefathers and foremothers have known and felt it. They wrote about it long before our time[3, 4] and it has been an integral part of various religious beliefs:

8000 B.C.

Animism (no separation between the physical and spiritual world; we are one in the energy)

2000 B.C.

Polytheism (multiple)

800

Monotheism (only one god)

1536

Reformation (more free faiths)

1776

Deism (God who does not intervene because the world is created perfectly in the energy)

1859

Scientific Materialism (only the physical world exists; there is nothing supernatural, like energy)

1901 - 1905

Max Planck and Albert Einstein develop formulae for energy and mass

1953

Discovery of DNA (cells on DNA strand, energy and ether are now known)

2003

All DNA sequences are mapped (energy and its impact at the cellular level can be measured)

2015

Holism (all senses are known and cooperate with energy, and we choose what we believe in)

When you're newly curious about how energy plays a role in our lives – and how it always has – it can help to think about the religious beliefs we know from Native American movies. It's rooted in animism and is all about nature's animating force. Animals, plants, and (for some) even non-living objects and phenomena contain a soul/spirit. There is no separation of the spiritual and physical world. Everything is one, and everything is energy.

Since then, there have been periods of shifting religious beliefs and, most recently, a long period where we have almost distanced ourselves from our soul life and celebrated materialism (what we can see) and the quantifiable and documentable (what we can measure). In other words, our perception of reality has changed remarkably over time (more on this in chapter 2).

Even though our ancestors found it natural, and even though the pendulum is actually swinging back towards a greater awareness of our soul life and individual existence in the Universe, we still struggle to understand that we are energy. In particular, we struggle to grasp that we are not only connected because we choose to connect with selected people. It is challenging to realise that we are all one – one energy field. Perhaps because we experience losing control and freedom or being insignificant in the grand scheme of things, even though it means the opposite, that we all matter to, are affected by, and affect the whole.

We have many ways of articulating it, such as believing in a God, that there was a Big Bang, and/or that I have a soul. Most people are aware of, or sense, that there is something bigger, some greater connection.

The period with a high degree of materialism that we are transitioning from has lasted since the 1600s and could also be called the mechanical period. It was characterised by great inventions in the realm of physics, including concepts like the law of gravity, mass attraction, the motion of bodies, and the theory of relativity.

It was a period of scientific discoveries that kick-started industrialisation. At the same time, the holistic view of human beings took a back seat – consciously and unconsciously. We slowly lost connection to our body and soul as we were raised and trained to be in our heads because that's what created "value", especially in the Western world.

Unfortunately, the rest of the world has copied the Western trend, which has resulted in us all feeling like soul amputees. We are missing our soul, and we must now learn to reconnect with it – although, of course, this is not easy after more than 500 years of being shaped by a culture that celebrated measurable and proven knowledge.

We are now entering a period of more spirituality, aided by concrete quantum physics discoveries to better understand that body, mind and soul are universally influenced and connected by energy frequencies.

We know, demonstrably, that we are energy. Everything on the planet consists of energy made up of atoms (energy in motion). All people, animals, things, plants, buildings, everything is made up of energy. Our energies overlap and blend, so everyone is connected. We are one big energy web.

Each person is an energy field with their personal frequency based on their DNA [5]. We affect and are affected by what happens around us in the energy web with our frequency. The really good news is that we can also influence our own energy field and frequency and, thus, the overall energy web.

This has two consequences:

- We are anything but insignificant in the grand scheme of things
- We can create our own happiness and health

The realisation of the latter is especially a cause of frustration for many leaders. Employees have discovered their own agency, importance, and responsibility for their well-being. They have discovered that the frequencies they are surrounded by daily are crucial to their happiness, health and ability to fulfil their potential and let their work positively impact the world.

You could say that you attract what you are:

- If we have negative thoughts, feelings and beliefs, we pull down the frequency of our energy field.
- Conversely, if we have positive thoughts, feelings and beliefs, we pull ourselves up in frequency.

In the same way, many have recognised that our surroundings have a frequency that is contagious:

- If we surround ourselves with negatively charged news, conversations, and tasks (which are also disguised thoughts, feelings and beliefs), we pull down the frequency of our energy field.
- On the other hand, if we surround ourselves with positive news, meaningful tasks, optimism and joy, we pull ourselves up in frequency.

Perhaps we haven't yet used the words energy and frequency to describe the phenomenon. But we have all experienced entering a room and immediately being attracted to another person on the same frequency, but not to those not on our frequency. In everyday speech, we talk about being on the same "wavelength". We are tuned into the same channel.

So we know. We're just unaware that we're all connected in such a way. And we lack the language to describe energetic (self-)leadership. These are virtues we have forgotten to cultivate whilst in the excitement of new knowledge and new achievements in the material world.

Science has actually been striving to prove the existence of ether (energy), which connects everything, since 1881. Albert Michelson and Edward Morley tried in 1887, and Bohr and Einstein in the early 1900s. Einstein concluded that there had to be something connecting everything. But he couldn't prove it.

On December 14, 1900, physicist Max Karl Ernst Planck presented a revolutionary theory to the German Physical Society in Berlin on the importance of frequency for our energy level:

> **Energy E = Planck's constant h** *denotes the effect of energy times time, the limit at which classical mechanics must be replaced by a quantum mechanical description of nature[6]) * **frequency f** (the frequency at which light oscillates)*

In English, the higher the vibration frequency, the more energy is created.

This knowledge was later built on by other researchers. Albert Einstein presented a formula in an article published on November 21, 1905[7]:

> **Energy E = mass m –** which is directly proportional to the square of the speed of light in vacuum * c^2

Or slightly more English:

> Rest energy E = mass * (speed of light)^2

Mass and frequency are, therefore, related. The result of Einstein's investigation is that energy and mass are the same thing.

The formula implies that a body with mass possesses energy even if it is at rest. At the same time, energy increases as mass increases. Thus, we can conclude that when we increase our frequency, we take up more space in the room and the universe, and we increase our energy. We have more to create from.

Your mass (energy field) increases when you raise your energy

You raise your energy by increasing your frequency

This means that the power is yours. You can change your frequency, and the higher the frequency your cells vibrate, the more energy you have. And the more you impact the world.

But even though it is the energetic coherence that we need the next hundred years to understand and align our lives with, you will see in this book that there is plenty we can do – yesterday.

We must learn to understand, feel and read our energy:

- to **feel** the present with our bodily brain
- to **listen** to the future with our energetic brain
- to **see** the future with our mental brain
- to **believe** in the future with our spiritual brain

When we manage to be conscious of the energy – feeling, listening, seeing and believing – we are much better able to take the right actions to adjust our change competency and advocacy skills.

The Energetic Leadership Model

Einstein helps us see that our job is to bring the human into our way of being in the world anew. We must, therefore, train and evolve constantly in our lives here on earth. We will never finish. Our "mission" here is arguably to learn to be human.

The Energetic Leadership Model is based on the ideal of infinite human potential and learning by *looking inwards* and *creating outwards*. It is also based on the interconnectedness of people and the world in a vast, indivisible energy grid, where we use our agency and intuitive sense in unison to set the intention for the future. By using intention from a balanced standpoint, we tap into our soul and stand strong at our core.

We must change the meaning of learning and the way we learn. Learning is also to draw on memories biologically inherited in our cells through our lineage, as well as experiences we have had ourselves. It is the sensations we receive and feel. Intuition that creates the voice of the soul. Our gift.

Learning starts from within, with what we feel, hear, see, and believe. Learning starts with awareness and wisdom that hasn't necessarily found its way to the external yet.

The Energetic Leadership Model[8] consists of two infinity signs, one vertical and one horizontal, which meet at the centre.

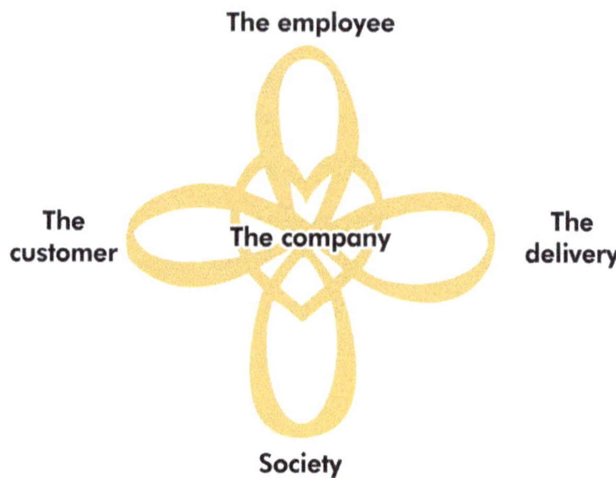

The vertical part of the model is about us as individuals in an organisation, whether we act as an employee or a professional manager. We are all leaders in our own lives. Because work is such an essential part of our lives, the company creates many positive or negative societal consequences in the 'use' of its employees.

I postulate that yesterday's management practices create far too many unintended, negative consequences, both for the individual and society, and that there is a vast potential to unlock by starting leadership from within and creating outwards.

The horizontal part is about having a business with a commercial or charitable purpose and the rhythm of such organisations. Just as our values have changed in the employee role, they have also changed in the customer role. We demand that companies enable us to contribute positively to a healthy and harmonious planet and a good life for our fellow humans through the deliveries and services we purchase.

The infinity sign symbolises an infinite development in the sign's true meaning. But also, there is a circular movement where we don't know the start and end point, where patterns are repeated, and where things, tasks, and people come back – in the same form and new forms.

Where the two signs meet is the centre of Energetic Leadership for both the individual and our relationship with ourselves, people close to us, and the community at large. From this centre emanates the energy to create the future we want.

Change competence lies in both horizontal and vertical development and has three learning stages:

- Technique (which is *what* you can do)
- Method (which is *how* you will do it)
- Persistence (which is the *routine* with which you will implement)

The three learning stages are a familiar invention. What's new is what we focus on and what knowledge resources we use. What we train comes from a genuine place and happens authentically. We must crack the code to change our competence in this way, like the curious people we are. When we crack it and find our true calling, we also find what makes us unstoppable and helps us put our creative power to work with both pleasure and ease.

What is your starting point?

Before you read on, I'd like you to think about your mindset.

- Are you curious about the future and how you and your organisation can grow into it?

- Are you frustrated by the stagnation, meaninglessness and disconnected leadership?
- Do you get annoyed and/or indignant when interacting with your partner or boss, or how people talk to each other?
- Is performance important to you, or are you more concerned with the process?
- Do you get angry about what's happening in the world, in the supermarket, at school, at work and in education.

All these thoughts and feelings are a good starting point for change because they indicate that something is bothering you. Something gets to you. There is something to work on both for yourself in terms of what you want to create, your relationships with others, and your collaboration.

Psychologist Carol Dweck has developed a fantastic and straightforward model called 'Fixed or growth mindset'.[9] [10]

If you have a **fixed mindset**, you often react in a passive, retreating or aggressive way when faced with challenges, obstacles, hardships, criticism, and success. Interestingly, we do this to maintain or stimulate others' perception of us as intelligent. But we don't grow and learn. And we don't create optimally in the world around us.

On the other hand, if you have a **growth mindset**, you like to embrace challenges. You like to keep going even in the face of adversity. You see hard work and difficulty merely as the path to knowing something (new) – that you have learnt something. You like to receive and learn from criticism or feedback. And you also find inspiration in the success of others. Here, the true potential is more likely to be realised.

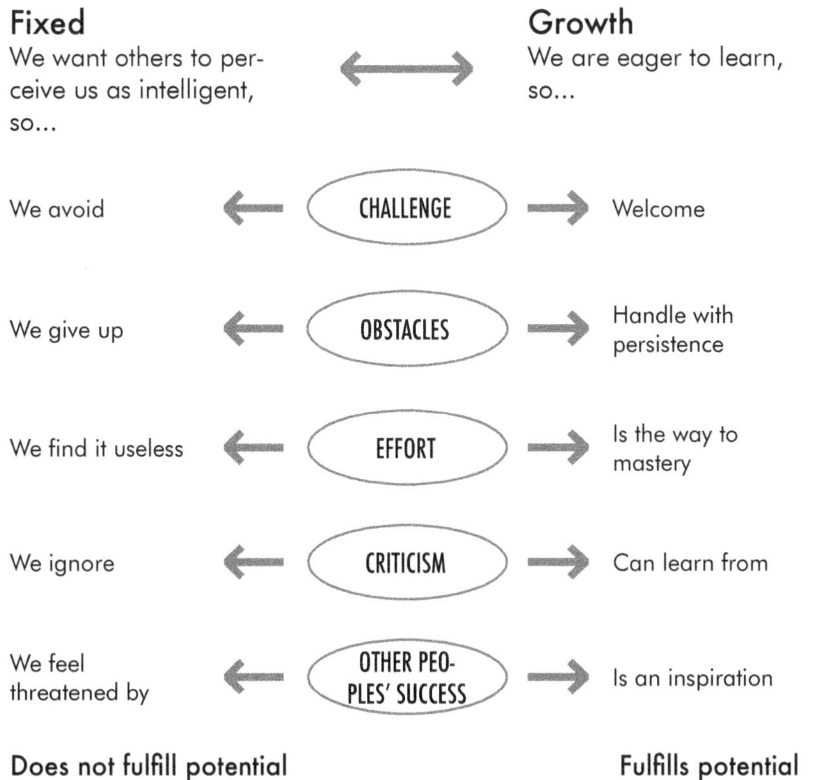

Is your mindset primarily fixed or growth-oriented?

Here are a few questions to help you answer that:

- How do you react when others have a different opinion?
- How do you react when others come up with a different idea than the one you just proposed?
- How do you feel when others are successful?
- What do you most often think about others – is it positive or judgmental?
- How do you react when something unexpected happens?
- How do you think your blind spots and shadow sides are expressed?

Playground Ltd

A fictive case study, Playground Ltd. describes several common symptoms in businesses today and how they may unfold in the future. I encourage you to reflect on how many of them are present in your company or how many seeds may have been sown to end up in the same situation.

Fictive Playground Ltd. is a technology company that produces IT equipment for various industries. It was established in 2013. Now, in 2033, we look back at how a severe crisis threatened the company's existence in 2023 and what it took to save it.

For the first 10 years of the company's life, all was well. The business was growing, employees were engaged, and customers were happy. It was fun to help build the company's success riding the wave of the financial boom that followed the financial crisis.

But gradually, growth slowed down. Absenteeism increased. Employees sought new pastures. Some, their very own pastures, as independents. Management was puzzled because they had just finished creating solid structures, had procedures for almost everything, a strong customer base, a booming tech industry and a healthy financial bottom line.

Despite that, employees were fleeing the business. Management couldn't figure out what to do and how to do it. Crises were everywhere, both in the outside world and inside the company.

Everyday life now mainly consisted of firefighting and crisis meetings. The new canteen scheme and two extra vacation days a year for staff hadn't helped the mood either. It was as if the creativity and spirit of the first 10 years were gone. It was as if a meltdown was happening that couldn't stop – a bit like the ice at the poles.

Occasionally, the group of managers joked that at least it was the difficult employees who were disappearing, and several times, work was set in motion to redefine vision and strategy.

One day at the cafe latte machine, the owner met Lisa from product development. She barely saw him but stood there sighing loudly. He gently asked if she was okay. She looked up, straightened her back and said: "No, not really – it doesn't make any sense what we're doing."

It turned into a long talk in the owner's office. And a walk together later in the week. More walks with other employees. Finally, there was somebody – also in management – who dared to look at the situation with a genuine interest in learning more and facing the unpleasantness.

Management had lost touch with how the mindset and needs of customers and workers had changed. With whether employees believed in the vision and strategies at all. And with themselves and their passion. The company's culture was not at all aligned with the needs of the future, the employees and the customers.

When the overdue conversation started in the group of managers, it turned out that they could indeed all feel it in the company, and most could also feel it in themselves. Several of them had even considered whether it was time to find something else to do. For many years, they hadn't dared to talk about the elephant in the room, but instead, they'd talked a lot about new products, sales and how they would create growth by reaching new markets. They were almost always looking outwards, not inwards.

They finally sat down, dared to talk about it all, and eventually dared to go with what they could actually feel themselves. They each chose to listen to their inner self, look behind the emotions, and believe and trust more that they had the right answers themselves and that it was essential to open up and listen to the inner lives of employees. What do we actually want? Why haven't we listened? What have we been afraid of?

It was a relief to say out loud what they felt, thought, sensed and experienced – and discover that no one was alone. Suddenly, shoulders dropped, trapped bile came out, and it was possible to breathe again.

A good example is that through improved dialogue between employees, the company increased interest in each other's areas of expertise, making it easier to step in during illness. The self-led teams took pride in delivering on their promises to the whole.

The company changed significantly, and the management task was approached in a radically different way. Among other things, it consisted of looking at the premise of their lives and, thus, also their leadership. They recognised that the price of ignoring the warning signs is far too high. When unhappy or unhealthy, energy is low and constipated, and it's the opposite when happy and thriving. Low energy creates low numbers on the bottom line.

All managers, employees, customers, and partners were involved in relaunching the company, and outside help was also brought in. Not for rational analysis but for advice and to learn how to listen inwardly, connect with their souls, and find the places where systems and processes had been inappropriately created and blocked energy. It was much more about personal development than business development, and everyone found it thought-provoking how much influence personal aspects had on the business.

They became aware that they didn't really have a language for what they were supposed to do and how it should feel to work in the company. They needed to find the language for new leadership, values, and principles and update their purpose, vision, and mission. They also had to find new ways to organise and collaborate. They had to learn to talk about things, even if it wasn't always comfortable.

In 2033, the company has a flat structure with 450 employees who are primarily self-led, in a cool way, leading from within and in touch with heart, soul and purpose, but still with a clear direction and framework.

The company has learnt to unleash its energy consciousness. It recognised that something much bigger was at stake than what the company was really about – producing tech equipment. When seen from a larger perspective, what the business was about grew in everyone's consciousness.

They understood that the inner drives the external development. They developed an entirely new culture based on energy and psychological safety derived from company and individual life purposes, coupled with a framework for self-learning and supported by a healthy use of technology.

Key questions were:

- How do we create a new leadership?
- How do we unleash our (everyone's) energy consciousness?
- How do we find our purpose and soul?

What Playground Ltd. has done is something every company can do:

- They work 30 hours a week.
- They have a flat structure with fewer managers, and the managers that are there work together across the board.
- They are aware of the importance of self-care, including daylight, calm breathing, sleep, diet, exercise, meditation, etc. So much so that they inspire and mentor each other.
- They are somewhat of a role model in the industry, and it has motivated them all to keep going when times are tough.
- Everyone has improved significantly physically, mentally and spiritually, and many can't understand how they had such a psychologically unsafe culture in the past and how much pressure they allowed their personal lives to be under.

Every person and every company can work with energy and its resolution. It's the most natural part of ourselves – we've just forgotten. We need to let go of the notion that we can change in an upward curve:

- Playground Ltd. is no longer the same team. There have been replacements, and some have resigned. But those who are there now are strongly attached to the company and the common purpose.
- Revenue dipped but is back and rising, and all three bottom lines are shining

There will always be external crises, but even in a storm, what you can control is intact. Your production and contact with customers. Connection with your employees. Connection with yourself. We are almost 100% in control of this – or at least we are in control of the practices and culture we create around it.

Some of the results you can expect are that attracting and retaining customers is easier, and absenteeism and medication consumption. All three bottom lines increase. You don't need to measure well-being but feel and talk about energy. Also, being part of a company where your life purpose aligns with the company's is something you talk about at job interviews and throughout your employment.

CHAPTER 2

Trends

From something to something else

We divide trends into megatrends and other trends. Megatrends[11] are trends that apply to all of us around the world. They represent such fundamental changes that they start several new related trends in a domino effect.

The 15 current global megatrends are closely related and are divided into 4 domains:

Global

1. Globalisation
2. Rising population
3. Environmental change and sustainability

People and society

1. An ageing world
2. Individualisation and empowerment
3. Focus on health
4. Urbanisation

Technology and science

1. AI and automation
2. Biotech revolution
3. Greater digital connectedness
4. Technological advances

Economy

1. Network Economy
2. Service Economy
3. Economic growth
4. Concentration of wealth

Other trends may be specific to a particular industry or area. The trends included in this book are those relevant to a company, organisation, NGO, or foundation – and to all of us as leaders and individuals. These trends relate to personal behaviour, opinion formation, values, and business management. Some may turn out to be global megatrends, but they are not yet.

A trend is an overview of a transition from one thing to another. We also call them from-to trends, and their style makes them great for communicating something complex in an easy-to-understand way. What is this shift that is changing us as a society, organisations, and individuals, and what are the consequences?

We often get caught up in everyday life and cope with the most urgent, the easiest to understand and what we know how to fix. However, one of the most important things for leaders is to be able to predict the future.

Working with trends creates a shared understanding and a common language. But it requires us to use all our senses and gain a deep understanding of what drives the trends that change our mentality, priorities, innovation and implementation capabilities and prompt us to relearn forgotten skills.

It's not in reports and development in numbers (knowledge) that we find gold. It's in the meaning we form around it. And if we wish to exchange gold for diamonds, this meaning must emerge from our inner self and our soul's true desires. Only then can we reject becoming subjects to other people's agendas (and egos) but instead take the helm and realise our full potential.

A good exercise after reading this book could be to consider whether there are trends other than the ones mentioned that affect your and your organisation's well-being and that you should also address and act on.

From industrial to planetary

The first trend is a fundamental and value-based shift in our industrial society, which paints a picture of a new way of doing business, a new way of being a leader, and a new way of being a participant in society.

Industrialisation has focused on efficiency and maximum output, almost at any cost – even if we had to first create a need for what we were good at producing cheaper or better.

We are currently in the midst of the fourth industrial revolution[12,13] :

1. Mechanical production (1784 - 1869)
2. Mass production (1870 - 1968)
3. Efficiency through electronics and IT (1969 - 2011)
4. Connectivity through cyber-physical systems (2012 and expected 20-30 years ahead)

According to leading futurologists, the ongoing fourth revolution will not be replaced by a fifth industrial revolution but by a more holistic and value-based revolution, which is already well underway, in parallel with the more technologically driven connectivity revolution.

In Chapter 1, we have historically looked back at our relationship with the energetic. The phases we presented also represented a shifting focus on spirituality and materialism. Suppose we plot these shifts onto a timeline with the two as the extremes. In that case, it becomes clear that the curve has a predictable trajectory and that now, and in the years to come, we will have a strained relationship with over-consumption and be more concerned with spirituality.[14] In fact, it has been 70 years since we peaked materialism in the 1950s. It's also worth noting that we peaked in spirituality around the year 800. It's no wonder we need to relearn how to deal with it.

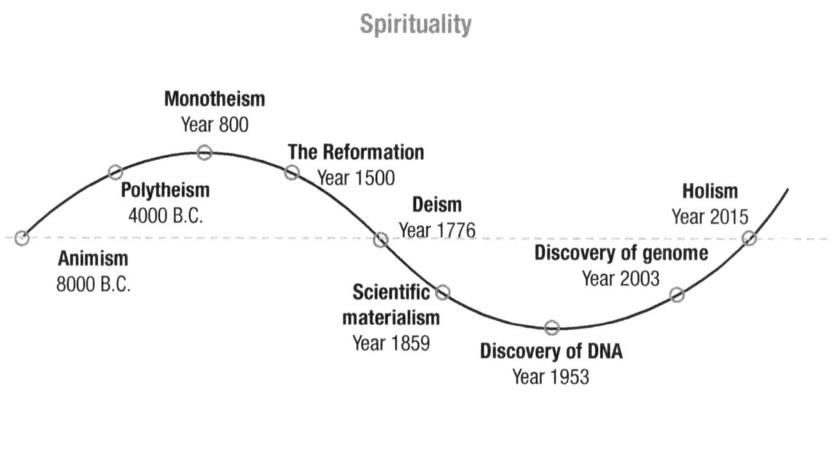

We are now heading towards a state where we are even more ready to sacrifice materialism, overconsumption, overproduction and unsustainable production. Today, we have a more holistic view of production. We are increasingly making demands on companies, both as customers and employees, because it's no longer about fair trade, child labour, rainforest clearance and good behaviour in general (although these are all important enough). Something much bigger is at stake: ensuring the survival of humanity and the planet.

> *Future is an act of rebellion*
> *if we challenge the future that is*
> *being presented to us*
> *by creating a more desirable vision*[15]
>
> **- DTU Skylab**

Planetary considerations have been absent to such an extent that we realise that more than sustainability is needed. Fortunately, many businesses also see the economic potential in the circular economy (which focuses on viability and recycling). However, neither of these perspectives has a sufficient focus on the need for planetary restoration and perhaps not enough focus on the inner restoration of the human being, which must change our behaviour as technical solutions evolve.

The future is about reinventing ourselves and the world we live in by coming up with proposals for a better world.

Now	**The Future**	**Desired future**
Sustainability	Circular	Regeneration
Do the least harm	Design out waste	Restore

From more to better

For the past 70 years, it's been about outward success and having or getting 'more'. It's been about bigger houses, more cars, more travel, more food and drink, more clothes, more gadgets, more open-space kitchens, etc. But with the increasing planetary and spiritual/holistic focus, we've also realised that more stuff doesn't make us happy.

We worry about leaving the planet behind, but we're also no longer willing to run faster and faster and then spend it all in half the time. We have realised the connection to the most valuable things we 'own': time and relationships. We have realised our duty to both the whole and the immediate.

We need to focus on 'better' rather than 'more'. Having better houses, better clothes, things that last longer. Better production, better waste management, better utilisation of resources and less food waste. 'Better' is the desire to focus on quality and the real impact of overconsumption on ourselves and the world around us. Earth Overshoot Day [16] (the day a country has used all its resources for the year) is 2nd August 2024 for the whole world; for the US, it's 14th March; for Germany/Ireland, 2nd May; for Argentina/South Africa, 20th June; and for Equador/Indonesia, 24th November. Obviously, it ought to be at the end of December or not reached at all.

This trend deeply resonates with consumers in the Western world. Being a part of it carries a sense of status, while there is no status in continuing consumption beyond what is necessary. Now we should only buy what we need. For some, there are strong emotions involved, such as fear, anger, worry and powerlessness. The meaning of life and the right to the planet are at stake. For others, in both the Western and non-Western world, this can be difficult to relate to when simply wanting better living conditions than your parents.

From conformist to rebel

As human beings in society and organisations, we have been used to having to adapt to a system. We could probably be allowed to turn a few knobs here and there and dust the corners to be able to do our job in the best possible way, but we have had (and in many places still have) very little influence on the basic structures and on how the work made sense, if at all.

We're simply not interested in that anymore. As we've reached the self-actualisation level of Maslow's Hierarchy of Needs, we've realised that life is too short to be spent meaninglessly. And we've realised that we don't have to put up with it anymore. We don't have to live so much of our day and life disconnected from our desires or who we are.

We miss being and being listened to, and we miss co-creating. What we are experiencing is an almost worldwide crisis of well-being deeply rooted in trauma and addiction (at least in the Western world). In recent years, we've even seen a whole new phenomenon emerge: the great resignation. People simply quit their jobs if it's not motivating and meaningful.

To a large extent, we're also seeing what we call quiet quitting or quiet resignation. Lots of employees (and managers) keep a low profile and do the job reluctantly and out of powerlessness over[17]:

- Lack of flexibility and career opportunities
- Not being valued as an employee

- Lack of understanding of the importance of self-management
- Declining organisational trust – 58% of employees surveyed in an HBR study trusted a stranger more than their manager[18]

We can find the reasons for this in inadequate leadership:

- Failure to deliver on promises
- No prioritisation of workplace culture
- Lack of focus on employee well-being
- Lack of focus on diversity and inclusion
- Failure to create meaningful work opportunities

On top of that comes employees who deliberately take an extended break and allow themselves to recharge, allow time for reflection, and allow time for pursuing things in life other than work.

Currently, there are four very different generations in the labour market. A surprising number of organisations have no plans for how to manage generational change – and very few consider the cultural change associated with generational differences.

The discussion quite often centres around young and old, inexperienced and experienced. However, we need a basic understanding that young people are not just younger – they represent the trend and mindset we are all moving towards. So, let's take a quick look at how the generations have been trained to think and what their priorities have been.

* * *

Baby boomers were born in the period 1945 to 1960 in the Western world. They have been more affluent, more active, and more physically fit than any previous generation and were the first to grow up with a clear anticipation that the world is constantly becoming a better place.[19]

This is a generation characterised by productivity. After the war, things needed rebuilding, so you had to be productive and contribute. Despite this, baby boomers have often been criticised for practising a consumer culture bordering on greed.

→ Their hope was *job security*

Generation X is from 1961-1980. As children of the 1970s and 1980s, during a time of social upheaval, Gen Xers were sometimes known as latchkey kids because they were not supervised by adults as much as previous generations and often had to lock themselves into their homes after school. This was in part due to an increase in divorce rates and women's increased activity in the labour market before out-of-home childcare became commonplace.

Researchers describe middle-aged Gen Xers as active and happy with a good work-life balance. There are many entrepreneurs among Gen Xers, the last generation for whom higher education has been a financial gain.[20]

→ Their aspiration has been a *work-life balance*

Generation Y was born between 1981 and 1995. They are also known as Millennials because they were children/young people around the turn of the millennium when disciplining children was not about firmness, staying quiet and obeying orders but more about creating an inclusive and appreciative environment. This generation didn't have to follow in the footsteps of their parents and was told that the world was open to their talent. It was just a matter of finding their right place. This has created a lot of optimism and high expectations, which have been hard to fulfil at times as the world has proved to be much more complex.

This generation is characterised by having grown up with computers, mobile phones and the internet and – as the first generation – naturally navigates the digital world. Social networking online is, therefore, also natural for them. It's a generation that craves recognition and doesn't listen to authority – sometimes manifesting itself in more sensitive behaviour and a stronger need for social relationships.

→ Their hope is *freedom and flexibility*

Generation Z, born from 1995 to 2010, are known as digital natives. With 9/11 in 2001, the fight against terror has been a part of Generation Z's life and upbringing, and being children during the 2008 financial crisis, some may have experienced parents or close family members losing their jobs. As a result, this age group has become moderate, conscious of their costs, and very pragmatic. They are also well-informed – they know what's going on and often have strong opinions that they expect others to take seriously. They engage in discussions about complex social issues, are inquisitive and can flexibly develop new opinions as information changes. They are also demanding and have high expectations of brands and products.

Living in a culture of perfectionism, where young people generally expect a lot from each other and society, can be tough. There is an increase in mental health disorders such as anxiety, stress and depression for this generation compared to previous generations. This may also be due to their parents' long working hours to make ends meet.[21] [22]

→ Their hope is *security and stability*

Generation Alpha was born in 2010 onwards, and naturally, their characteristics, values, and behaviours say a lot about what we can anticipate in the future. The technological, social and educational trends that are currently influencing Alphas in their formative years will affect their future behaviour and, indirectly, their parents. The generations are not just different as groups. More precisely, they are at various stages of development towards the same new world.

To a certain extent, Generation Alpha demonstrates the same behaviours, attitudes and beliefs as Millennials, but their more complex family structure, combined with the technological and social development happening, means that they are not simply clones of their parents. They are used to a world that is tailor-made for them, shaped in an age of individualisation and customisation, and where Netflix predicts exactly what they want to watch next.

Generation Alpha is perhaps the most socially isolated generation to date. Countless academic reports have shown that social media makes people feel less connected, resulting in a greater sense of isolation and reduced life satisfaction. One of the consequences is that they will seek out services and brands that make them feel genuinely and authentically connected to others. And they will seek workplaces that are inclusive and where there is a shared meaningful purpose.

It will take them longer to grow up and become contributing citizens who help provide for and create in our society. A master's degree is now standard, and as a result, a Ph.D. is becoming more common. Generation Alpha is staying in school longer, pushing responsibilities of adulthood – and purchasing power – further into the future.

Both educational institutions and organisations that sell and communicate to Alphas need to ensure that the job, product and communication are tailored to the individualism that is part of their DNA.

→ Their hope is *individuality and authenticity*

* * *

Looking ahead to 2030, the boomers will have retired, and we will have a global labour market that looks like this:[23]

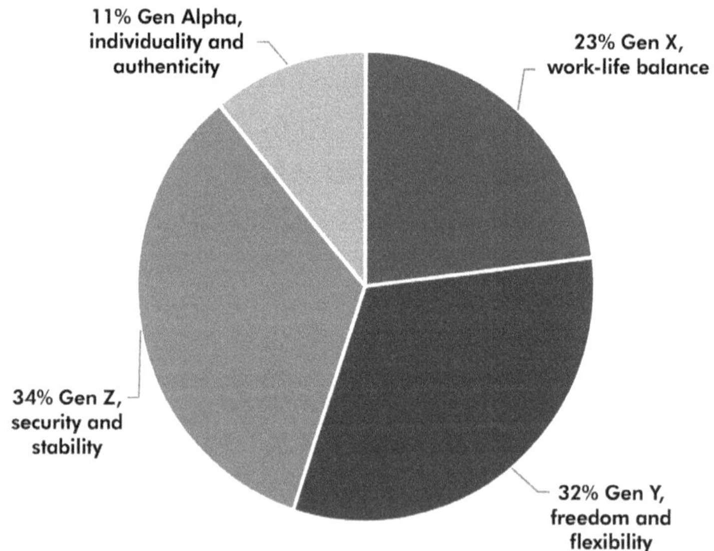

We'll have a labour market that's no longer particularly concerned with efficiency, productivity and growth for the sake of profit. The characteristics of the generations from Baby Boomers to Alpha are evoking with increasing clarity human beings who are individualists, expect customised products and services, and crave authenticity in their social relationships.

In the past, there was a specific career path to follow, adapting to the same career path and ladder as colleagues, continuously pursuing the next promotion for the sake of power, status and pay grade. It is said that in the future, Generation Z will have 6 careers and 18 different jobs. The well-defined career ladder and long seniority are dead.

In response, we're redefining what a career actually is and busy figuring out what we want for ourselves. What is my calling? Sure, we still like a good salary. But not if the price is to live in disharmony with our values or the work is meaningless. There is also no longer a correlation between good pay and following a predefined career path. Often quite the opposite.

Careers in the industrial society were also solely linked to one's paid work. In the new communal society, a career will be a mix of paid work, voluntary work, family and private life, based on what creates meaning, that is, if we don't skip the term career altogether. Meaning is personal, and therefore, career as a concept might disappear and be replaced by one's life path.

When working for a meaningful cause is more important than a so-called career, it means that leaders need to be very aware of and able to find a connection between the rebel's desires (who will shortly be the majority) and the purpose of the organisation, its values and strategy.

We no longer just want to be someone who adapts to the system, being a conformist. We don't even see ourselves as rebels anymore if we go out of our way to make demands because the time we're in is in favour of the natural in everyone living up to their true potential. The "dinosaurs" saw spirituality as rebellious, but in the new age of energetic leadership, it's a prerequisite – a hygiene factor.

The strongest desire to create something new is seen in the rebels who quit their jobs and want to create something new, breaking out in all sorts of ways. They are the frontrunners who show a way out of the madness, and as the generations are pushed forward in time, baby boomers retire, giving more space to the more rebellious generations X and Y. It's no longer a case of a single "disgruntled" or "unhappy" employee here and there. It's an actual cultural shift.

To avoid reaching a point where the most progressive employees leave the company, it's important to emphasise that they don't leave the company because they don't want to work. On the contrary. Rebels love to create and develop, and they often have a strong desire to change and develop the organisation itself to make it more future-proof and innovative, make work more meaningful, and have fun at work.

From conformist - to rebel

I adapt to the workplace	→	the workplace adapts
It feels hard (doing something meaningless)	→	it feels difficult (learning new things I want to do)
Unconscious mindset	→	conscious mindset
Same types of profiles	→	different types of profiles
Culture characterised by group pressure	→	culture characterised by cooperation
Culture freezes out people who want change	→	culture prioritises people who want the new leadership and community
Little respect for the right to exist	→	high respect for the right to exist
Learning to know	→	learning to learn
Knowledge	→	wisdom

From retirement to breaks

We want a life that's not like our parents' life. Previously, you worked for 40-50 years, then retired, then died. The pension is about three generations old and belongs to the industrial society, not the late modern society we live in now (also known as the service society). [24]

The retirement rebellion

- The dawn of time: Work or die
- Ancient times: You can grow old as long as you are a man
- 1880s: The pension is invented
- 1910s: Life is getting longer (medical advances)
- 1920s: Old is boring
- 1935: You are forced with money to retire
- 2. World War: They want you back again
- 1950s: Live strong, die young
- 1970s: Youth rebellion, women's right to work
- 1980s: Individualisation and new freedom
- 1990s: The information society
- 00s: Financial crisis and anxiety
- 10s: Rebellion simmers, and now we have social media to find the other rebels and share the knowledge they tried to hide from us
- 20s: Global instability fuels the rebellion of rebels – young, adult and old alike. We want to live while we do – and ensure our children can do the same.

We want meaning and to truly contribute. Our education and training are endless. And we want it both in our working lives and leisure time. We want flexibility and the freedom to choose what we work for. And we still want to be active when we grow old.

Author and PhD Ingrid Giese has both researched and written about the phenomenon. Her book "Opting In and Out" (2018) has a particular focus on women's behaviour concerning identity, culture and career models. Still, Giese's research is primarily about how both men and women act to create sustainable lives, work lives and careers in a world that is moving from masculine dominance to a better balance by stepping out or away and creating either their own path or influencing others in a better direction.

You can say that retirement has been cancelled. That is, we don't want retirement the old-fashioned way, where we're old when we get to take time off (and be called a burden). Instead, we want a life where we have continuous longer breaks, life breaks, where we can live, educate and fulfil ourselves while we are healthy.

Pension companies and governments must rethink what a pension should actually be like in the future because we don't want the old model. Being the rebels that we are, we find solutions ourselves and are happy to withdraw our pension early in order to fulfil our dreams and live what we consider to be the good life.

The old model is simply dead. In fact, we don't want anyone – not even our employer – to interfere with how much we save or who we trust with our pension savings. We don't need a pension system. We need a break system that supports us to learn, perform, enjoy, and nourish ourselves until we retire the colourful dancing shoes and the golf clubs.

 As leaders, it's our job to figure out how to attract and retain employees in new ways when they no longer work for just one employer – checking in at the beginning of their career and then checking out fifty years later – but come and go at intervals. The company's strategy must take this into consideration and contain an attitude and actions on how the organisation will develop over the next decade.

There will definitely be things in that plan that have never been there before. The plan must consider that it was needed yesterday, as workers across the globe are already quitting their jobs if they can't go on leave to build a school in Nepal or write a book in Nairobi.

As citizens and participants in the society we create, we must also be more aware of what kind of income we have. Where would we like it to come from in the future? How do we ensure that we have the opportunity to take these breaks? How can we have more overlapping incomes and "passive" income?

It could be that we get them from both regular employment and from consultancy or freelance work. Or we could be self-employed or own multiple businesses.

It's also likely that as private individuals, we earn money from our homes because they can generate electricity. And rent out our car when we're not using it. And since we now prefer better to more, we might also want to live more modestly and buy less to afford the things that give life its true colour and meaning.

Our perception of how to make money will change in the future, and it's not just the few who will make these changes. It's the new normal to earn more in some periods than in others. That you invest. That you prioritise. Prioritise time and meaningfulness over norms and traditions, as we saw with the baby boomers who wanted job security and Generation X, who wanted stability in their work-life balance. This way of organising your life highlights the importance of knowing your true purpose in life.

From closed hierarchy to open communi-teams

Knowledge is no longer something that is poured from the top and dosed down the organisation. Knowledge is sucked in from all sides.

The industrial society and previous eras taught us that knowledge comes from above, from the church, the king, and the management. The need for liberation in recent decades, coupled with IT and digitalisation, has created a need and demand for us to navigate all the information surrounding us and act on it. We don't want to sit and wait to be given information but to be involved respectfully and in trust.

This trend is a detachment from the expert or the boss who knows everything. No one can know everything today, not even a CEO, prime minister or president. The hierarchical and often patriarchal rule of the willful and powerful leader has had its heyday. The new greatness as a leader consists precisely in being able to navigate turbulent seas calmly and with empathy and intuition in order to have the information needed to act, motivate, and make final decisions on a solid foundation.

Modern leadership is also about allowing yourself to be challenged on all your judgements and blind spots and surrounding yourself with employees who can help ensure that all necessary knowledge is brought to light because a safe, open and curious space has been created where intuition and intuitive knowledge and personal aspirations are also taken into account. At the same time, understanding and respecting the employee's need – to be able to navigate freely and safely and, thus, develop – is a significant incentive to stay affiliated with the organisation.

This requires management to trust the new generations and to listen and involve them. And it requires new generations to respect and trust their leaders in a human transformation that everyone finds demanding.

The hierarchical system is retreating, and we are moving towards a more circular and flat organisational structure that is more naturally shaped by our values, working principles, tasks, collaborations and partnerships. A system that can be built on 6 principles[25]:

1. Humanity
2. Changeability
3. Connectedness
4. Diversity
5. Development
6. Rhythm

We already see the flat structure in many, especially newer organisations. There is not one top manager, but perhaps one manager for every 100 people, who is more likely to lead from the ground up in a kind of facilitating role with self-managing teams. They often have fewer leaders than more established organisations traditionally have.

An organisation is also an organism of living beings that grow when they are watered and die when they are not nourished. They are beings with an inherent rhythm, in the same way nature has with its seasons and plants that sprout, bloom and die to be resurrected.

Unfortunately, many people today feel that we have created a society and organisations that assume it's summer all year round. There is no built-in hibernation and regeneration, where the nervous system can calm down and energy reawaken.

Trend researchers in cultural and organisational development now recognise that nature, people, relationships and energy are vital parts of businesses, society and the planet. For this reason, Frederic Laloux has published an addendum called "The Week"[26] to his culture model (from machine to family to circular).[27] The Week emphasises the need to come together, build relationships, get ideas, and support each other to expand and lift the energy to find the solutions we and the world need to be sustainable. I have experienced The Week myself and highly recommend it to create awareness and action and as a tool when facilitating your own groups.

Due to decades of focusing on optimisation through machines, data and IT, we have forgotten that people are the nerve centre of the organisational structure. We need to be able to interact in an easier and more human way that doesn't drain our energy. One prerequisite for this is that we can retrieve information without detours, build relationships and collaborate with the right people on tasks.

As Frederic Laloux says: "Our children will ask: What did you know? And what did you do?" More specifically, we can add: "What did you feel? Who did you listen to?"

From dominance to dualism

As humans, we consist of both feminine and masculine energy. It has nothing to do with being male or female, although a woman often majors in the feminine and a man often majors in the masculine by virtue of their gender. But when we talk about energies, we all have both, regardless of how we identify as a gender.

The masculine energy is located in the right side of the body (for the brain, however, the left hemisphere), often the strongest and most controlling side physically. Masculine energy is to have drive, be vigorous and take action. We are decisive.

The feminine energy is located in the left side of the body, where our heart is (for the brain, however, the right hemisphere). The feminine energy is that we listen and take the time to lean into the situation and be present, that we are reflective and empathetic and feel the present moment in the situation and the person in it. This is where our emotions, empathy and love stem from.

In popular speech, masculine energy is about "human doing" – a driving force in which people take action and do something. The feminine energy is about "human being" – a force that allows us to simply be and reconnect. For generations, masculine energy has been traditionally recognised in the workplace, while feminine energy was associated with the private sphere.

When there is harmony and balance between our masculine and feminine energies in our actions, we walk on two legs and live and act in a balanced way. You could also say that we use both our accelerator (masculine) and clutch (feminine).

Masculine energy

- Action-orientated
- Focused
- Progressive
- Straightforward
- Courageous
- Self-reliant
- Hardworking
- Strong
- Ambitious
- Proud
- Independent
- Vigorous

Feminine energy

- Being
- Creative
- Listening
- Affectionate
- Vulnerable
- Grounded
- Long-term
- Humble
- Curious
- Empathetic
- Team player
- Generous

The duality and flow of energy

The masculine is focused – the feminine is intuitive

The masculine acts – the feminine feels

The masculine seeks freedom – the feminine seeks love

The masculine is consciousness and order – the feminine is intuitive and chaotic

The masculine looks forward – the feminine is in the present moment

There is a rapidly growing awareness of these two distinct energies and a realisation that balance between them is fundamental to human functioning. We have had (have) a society where we have been very driven by the masculine, which means that we have walked on one leg. A human being can't do that for very long. Even if it's possible for a while, we're wearing ourselves out in all the wrong ways. Without a balance between the fundamental energies, humans are, at best, incapable and insufficient and, at worst, sick. We must be able to both be and act.

It's important not to confuse this trend of individual balance with the trend of gender politics. There is that, too, but that's about equity, diversity and inclusion.

From one to three bottom lines (ESG)

Throughout industrialisation, and indeed for many centuries, economics has been one of the most important factors in assessing whether we are doing well. We've measured everything important in money; the only bottom line was the financial bottom line.

The financial bottom line is still important. A healthy business requires a healthy financial bottom line in the black, not in the red. But as we've become more conscious of how we run our businesses and the impact it has on the resources that companies depend on (people and the earth's resources), we've come to realise that it's being done in a completely wrong way that benefits no one and has serious consequences. We see this especially in the form of the climate crisis, the biodiversity crisis and the crisis of human malaise.

The three bottom lines first saw the light of day in 1987 when the UN (The World Commission on Environment and Development) published the report "Our Common Future", also known as the Brundtland Report, as the former Prime Minister of Norway headed the commission. The report describes sustainability for the first time in terms of the social responsibility of all parties (governments, the public sector, the private sector and citizens) to contribute.

Sustainability is nothing new. Our forefathers and mothers knew about it; they didn't pick the last wild carrot, and they didn't pee in the river. They ensured new blood in their families. Now, the Brundtland report elevated it to something new to enforce focus on it so that we can better act with a united front.

The positive thing that has come out of the report is a common focus, including 17 concrete global goals created during 2012-2015, as well as a comprehensive foundation for goals and reporting. This focused work has resulted in what we today call the ESG goals: the climate, social and economic aspects, goals and benchmarks of being sustainable[28].

- **Environmental**: The environmental bottom line is about organisations' focus on climate change, e.g. carbon footprint, earth resources (including water and minerals), pollution and waste minimisation and management. In other words, we create and apply green solutions.

- **Social**: The social bottom line is about organisations' focus on human capital, e.g. human rights, health, diversity, safety, conflicts of interest, traceability, social opportunities (e.g. access to funding), and investment in the social part of the organisation.

- **Governance** (economics): The economic bottom line is about organisations' focus on corporate governance, such as leadership competencies, corporate behaviour, purpose, values, principles, strategy, ethics and transparency.

These proposals for goals and guidelines for how organisations can work to create change and report the impact are attracting much attention, especially since it is now mandatory for large companies and listed companies (accounting classes C and D) residing in the EU to submit an ESG report to their owners, board and auditors – and the public. In a few years, this will also apply to SMEs – small and medium-sized enterprises.

While these very ambitious and mandatory reporting rules on sustainability currently only apply to the EU, the UK and US are expected to follow. All countries outside the EU could be affected indirectly as European companies require suppliers to provide sustainability reports[29].

But we are not there yet.

The climate bottom line speaks volumes to us all, and it has finally made organisations focus on reducing their carbon footprint and finding new solutions. That is concrete sustainability that we can understand because we see, feel and are concerned about the concrete changes we observe in the world around us.

The social bottom line is perhaps the most poorly defined in relation to ESG goals and guidelines. The descriptions are still very externally focused and lack focus on how we can measure and report on internal sustainability at an organisational, managerial and employee level. Therefore, for many companies, the focus will be on the part that creates better external conditions and not on the internal. This is not enough to solve the crisis we are experiencing around human health and well-being.

The efficiency regime fails when the price is stress and workers practise active or quiet quitting. They no longer appreciate pseudo-work, philosopher Anders Fogh Jensen and anthropologist Dennis Nørmark postulate [30]. Generations X, Y and Z agree, saying they don't want meaningless roles and tasks that don't create value for themselves or the organisation, let alone for customers and citizens who experience an inadequate or slow customer experience. It's simply not motivating.

Today, we are good at measuring sickness absence and translating it into lost value. We are less good at measuring well-being, psychological work environment, engagement and utilisation of talent, and consequently, we lack awareness of the value it has for the bottom line. Put simply, we are very good at measuring the rational, tangible, and external areas, but we are less good at measuring the soft, relational, and internal areas.

This applies to both employees and customers. Significant amounts are spent on understanding and analysing customer needs and behaviour to generate business and a positive financial bottom line. Now, the time has come to do the same for employees so that the real social bottom line isn't constantly flashing red. It's time to realise that it's neither human nor financially free to stand idle in this area.

We need to create workplaces that feel more like playgrounds, where there is room for both an economic and a social bottom line – a human bottom line, where people understand how to create meaning for the company and themselves in a happy symbiosis.

Streamlining, making money, and measuring in money is fine. However, we also need to have an equally important bottom line that truly reflects the positive and negative results we produce. Just as we create positive or negative economic outcomes, our work in organisations also creates a positive or negative human outcome.

That actually brings us to the financial bottom line, which is about leadership and leadership behaviour, and the focal point of this book: how to create financially healthy results for organisations in new ways.

What's new for organisations is that it's no longer just a matter of gaining a competitive advantage. We simply won't buy their products or be employed by them if they don't act responsibly. The company's story – the narrative – is of paramount importance, and it's not enough to deliver financial statements with a healthy bottom line and satisfactory growth. What matters now is *how* they achieve their results. In other words, what leadership and management approach does the organisation practise? Here lies the key to success for the organisation and the future.

With the imperative demands for three bottom lines, reporting and governance have become a multidimensional task for management in many organisations, which doesn't make it any easier to be a leader. Everything intertwines with a responsibility, not just about the "small", almost controllable part of the value chain. No, management is now responsible for the entire multidimensional, circular value chain. That said, we also know that external crises such as COVID-19, wars and natural disasters will constantly challenge all three bottom lines.

From external to internal sustainability (first)

In recent years, new management has been provided with many adjectives, such as regenerative (being able to rebuild itself), sustainable, natural, balanced, conscious, ethical, moral, and transformational – all with the aim of changing the old way of managing to a new and better way. We need to take the long view and see the development of our health, society, and culture in a long-term view instead of a short-term view.

We focus a lot on sustainability, but generally, we don't really understand it fully. We don't talk sufficiently about the fact that there are actually two parts to it: outer sustainability and inner sustainability.

Outer sustainability is governed by our minds and knowledge, and that's what the 17 sustainable development goals (SDGs) address. It's about being carbon neutral, looking after our nature, and ultimately, biodiversity and our survival on the planet. We don't know how to succeed, and we're not doing nearly enough – but we do know what external sustainability is.

Inner sustainability is guided by our heart, soul and wisdom. None of the SDGs addresses inner sustainability, which is about joy – feeling good and living meaningfully and healthily in both the short and long term.

It's not really surprising that a strategy with 17 goals has been created for our outer world without addressing the inner world because we have been trained to understand with our heads and have suppressed how much we lack the connection to our heart and soul.

Managing with the head alone is too narrow-minded and technical an approach. It is inadequate, even though it is possible to achieve results to some extent – and perhaps even satisfy the boss, board and shareholders with great numbers on both the financial bottom line and the formal carbon footprint.

What many are beginning to realise is that our outward-focused strategies are inadequate and that we are seeing the consequences of this. We're starting to believe that we need to embrace the inner. We are realising that it's the inner that actually drives the outer.

What we have forgotten are the laws of nature. We have forgotten that man is nature and not a machine. We have forgotten what nature is at its core – planting a seed in nourishing soil, watering and nurturing it so that it grows big, beautiful and robust. That cells in animals and humans are designed to (re)build themselves, provided they live in a healthy environment.

We have forgotten to nurture and care for our own lives, ignoring the original fundamental laws of nature and the tools by which a healthy life is created and maintained through our senses. This realisation has a vital impact on how we can define effective leadership.

Future designer Stephan Grabmeier [31] emphasises this situation very well in the movement from VUCA to BANI, showing that we need to find a new path. The old leadership shoes are worn out and holey, and the new ones are made of a completely different multidimensional substance.

Stephan Grabmeier describes a development in our inner and soft values, which will become much more important in the future. These values will no longer be suppressed but become values and competencies that we will embrace in every way, as individuals and as a company.

The world goes from and to:

Volatile	→	Brittle
Uncertain	→	Anxious
Complex	→	Non-linear (multidimensional)
Ambiguous	→	Incomprehensible

A BANI world requires resilience and inner sustainability, humanity, adaptability, and the ability to "read" the future, as well as transparency and intuition. [32]

We must also seek greater insight into the characteristics of the customers we will actually have in the future because, of course, like our employees, they will be radically different from what we have been used to. Both in their values and their behaviour.

In the future, customers will focus on whether the company's internal and external narrative is coherent – also with what they deliver. For example, if a company says that a dining table is made from sustainable wood, the customer will want to see "proof" of this in the form of descriptions, track and trace, and certificates. This will reassure them that the supplier is being monitored to ensure the wood is verifiably sustainable. They want to know the environmental impact of the table's production.

Customers (and investors) will also pay much more attention to whether the company treats its employees well. Are people managed sustainably so that there are no inhumane conditions, both in terms of, ie. child labour, stress, and other malaise? And is there consistency in the narrative from the salesperson, the advert, reviews and mentions, and the financial statement with the three bottom lines?

We've come a long way in these areas. But not nearly far enough. How much more evidence do we really need before we listen to the inner voice shouting louder and louder, saying, "Do something else and something better! Nature is suffering! Too many people are sick and unhealthy! It can't go on any longer!"

We simply have to take seriously what we are already observing. Feel and listen inwardly to what we really want, see, and believe. Then, actively – and sometimes courageously – make it a central part of how we gain insight, our way of leading, our strategy, and how we financially manage the changes it requires. Plus, find the financial potential in an internally driven sustainability strategy.

For the individual, this means that we are now seeing people finally embracing courage and taking control of their own lives to a large extent – not only for their own happiness but also for the happiness of their workplace and, most importantly, for the happiness of the planet and the future.

In order to believe that change is possible, we must dare to feel what we actually feel. Dare to listen to what we hear. And dare to see what we actually see.

In the future, we will have an even stronger personal focus on our energy and awareness. Energy conservation will become a superpower – being able to create your own sense of security and replenish, dose, and find balance after fluctuations. We are increasingly seeking to create space to be quiet and listen inwards, to find answers, creativity, meaning and energy from within rather than from external, rational analyses.

Many have recognised this and are willing to start from within and then work with the results externally. This places new demands on leadership skills when employees start designing their lives first and, thereafter, the associated flexible, self-managing work life.

From automatic to AI-magical

Unfortunately, we often see that presence, energy and connection to people have disappeared in many buying and service situations. The price of automation should not be impersonality. According to Universal Futurist, in the future, we will expect a soul-led customised service that runs smoothly and automatically, giving us the coveted "wow experience".[33]

In many cases, the customer experience in the physical space has deteriorated over the past 20 years. Customer experience expert Ian Wisler-Poulsen says that development is speeding up professionally and technologically. Products and services are becoming more complex, and often, the customer doesn't have the professional skills to understand the service. Therefore, their judgement ends up being based on experience. For the same reason, experience is becoming more important to a company's strategy.

Over the past 50 years, we've automated and digitised – which has many benefits – and at the same time, we've collected and used increasingly more data about customers, their needs and processes. This has made us knowledgeable about what happens and when and especially how long it takes and costs in terms of money. In many areas, we have actually become very good at designing processes and automating and digitising them. In Denmark, self-service in the public sector and payment with the MobilePay app are examples of customer processes that have been significantly improved through technology but are now losing to global solutions. In the US, apps like Venom and Zelle are widely used, just like Apple Pay and Google Wallet have gained ground globally. In Asia, the Gojek app (here, you do not need a bank account to start using it) from Indonesia is spreading into Singapore and Vietnam.

The new and huge trend is artificial intelligence (AI), which can not only process the data we have or collect from the customer but also actively participate in, for example, creation processes and ideation. We don't want to be numbers in an automated system but have AI-magical experiences. We want the best of both worlds – a magical, personalised, and digitised experience. Suppose the robot that greets us at reception is empathetic, personalised and maybe even entertaining. In that case, chances are we won't feel like we're being subjected to automation but as recipients of an AI-magical experience.

AI has been around for a long time and is (even if we were unaware) integrated into many of the solutions we use in everyday life, especially in any context where it makes sense for a computer to aim at predicting what we want to do or say next.

This means that CX and IT developers working in collaboration have become more aware and adept at adding value from AI to the customer journey, citizen journey, employee journey, and the associated delivery across all customer, citizen and employee touchpoints.

In the autumn of 2022, ordinary people were able to access the open-source code behind most AI-supported systems: ChatGPT. This raised our awareness of the potential, possible ethical issues, and sweeping and lasting changes to millions of jobs to a whole new level. Before, many believed that AI primarily threatened blue-collar jobs. Now we're realising that it's very much a concern for all of us.

Our understanding of humans and technology and how they interact is constantly evolving, especially after the introduction of artificial intelligence. In this context, Maria Benedikte Skjærven from Danish Futurescouts proposes a 10th intelligence, human-machine interaction [34] (Chapter 3 briefly describes the other nine types of intelligence).

She writes in her newsletter: "In a time of constant technological development and digitalisation, it is necessary to understand and master the interaction between humans and machines. Focusing solely on prompt engineering or designing user interfaces is no longer sufficient. Instead, we should develop a deeper understanding of how humans and technology can work together and complement each other."

The 10th intelligence, human-machine interaction, encompasses a wide range of competencies and abilities, including understanding the difference between AI and traditional software, understanding the technology's limitations and potential, formulating clear and concise questions or instructions for AI, assessing AI answers for accuracy and relevance, and identifying any bias or errors in AI responses.

Undoubtedly, AI, along with new applications of blockchain technology, are the most significant game-changers to hit us all in this decade. We are thus facing a new era where these wide-ranging and disruptive changes force us to shine a spotlight on the human and ethical sides as well. We must not let this opportunity go to waste in digital transformation.

A magical customer experience in the future can take many different forms:

- Two or more people physically interact and look each other in the eye.
- A semi-automated experience where the customer, employee and machine together create the solution.
- A 100% automated experience where the customer alone activates the process and receives a predictable outcome.
- An AI magic experience, where the customer creates their own unique customer experience using artificial intelligence.

The latter can generate an incredible amount of energy and loyalty, and while there are ethical concerns, it's a whole new level of efficiency that has created a new enthusiasm for technology. Soon, using AI to create magical customer experiences will not be a real choice for business but a standard component that customers expect.

CHAPTER 3

The energetic human being

Old Me and New Me

Sometimes, it's easier to understand something that's big and complex when it's presented in a fun and simple way. This story covers the basic concepts of the body, mind, consciousness, ego, and soul.

Old Me and New Me are sitting on a bench on a beautiful spring day in 2033, talking about how much has happened in the last 10 years.

Old Me asks: When did it all start?

New Me answers: It all started when I realised I have an ego.

Old Me asks: What is an ego?

New Me answers: I didn't really know at the time either.

> **Ego** is Latin for 'I'. In philosophy and psychology, it is traditionally the centre of the personality to which consciousness and will are linked. Through the individual's experiences, a complex identity is built upon the ego through which the individual differentiates themself from others.[35]

New Me continues: Sometimes my ego is my good friend, sometimes my lousy friend.

Old Me: I don't understand. How can your ego be both your good friend and your lousy friend?

New Me: My ego is my good friend when we are good at getting things done together. But it's my lousy friend when my ego tries to make me do something I don't want to or can't do. Then I get sad, unhappy and angry.

Old Me: But you've become happier over the last many years, haven't you? How can that be?

New Me: I think it has something to do with my becoming more consciously aware.

Old Me: Conscious. What does it mean to be conscious?

New Me: Conscious awareness is knowing yourself and what's around you.

Old Me: Oh... That sounds interesting!

New Me: It is very interesting. It just requires you to be good at feeling, listening, and seeing what your body is telling you. Of course, it requires some training, but because it's fun, it doesn't feel like training. It's something I look forward to. It energises me.

Old Me: Can you tell me how you became more conscious and happy?

New Me: Yes, I am happy to. It was an important realisation for me that I had a good ego and a bad ego. It expanded my consciousness and made me start thinking about where I was happy in my life and where I wasn't. I realised that my bad ego has often had a lot of control over what I did and thought. And that made me sad. It feels a bit like being trapped inside yourself.

Old Me: What did you do not to feel so trapped?

New Me: I've become more aware of how I talk to myself. In other words, did I have good or bad thoughts about myself? I became more aware of what my mind is – how my thoughts affect my emotions and actions.

Old Me: Stop for a second before you go any further. I need to understand that. What is the mind?

New Me: Yes, it's good you ask because it's important.

> **The mind** refers to aspects of intellect and consciousness manifested by a combination of thought, sensation, memory, emotion, will and imagination. The mind is the flow of consciousness. The mind includes all the unconscious processes of the brain.[36]

Old Me: I get curious to know more. What did you do to work with your mind?

New Me: I've always played different kinds of sports, including swimming, tennis, and running. But in my gym, there was a yoga class with an amazing yoga teacher who was (is) yoga, and that's where I found the joy of yoga, both in its active and calm form.

Old Me: I know about yoga, but isn't it physical exercise?

New Me: Yes, it's physical exercise for the body and breath, but it's also good for the mind because yoga classes use silence, soothing sounds, and music that calm you down. I started to feel my body much better. And then yoga did another important thing. Along with my game changer.

Old Me: What is a game changer?

New Me: It can be an event that changes something significant in your life. For me, it was losing my job. But it was actually a good thing because I realised that I could do something better and different for myself, for others, and for the planet. It lit a spark in me. However, I had a hard time figuring out what that spark wanted until I got even better at listening to myself and what my heart wanted through my weekly yoga practices.

Old Me: But how can you actually listen to a heart? It's just an organ that pumps blood around.

New Me: Yes, you're right. I mean it in a figurative sense. You listen to your intuition or gut feeling. What is it that I really want? And not what my bad ego – my head – thinks is best.

Old Me: Well, New Me, I'm jealous. You have found your ego, your consciousness, your heart, your mind, and you train every day to feel and listen. And you do what you believe in. Phew. There can't be more.

New Me: Dear Old Me, it never really ends, and there's still a lot I have yet to tell you. Do you know what the soul is?

Old Me: Actually, I'm not sure I understand the difference between the mind and the soul. And how to recognise it?

New Me: I'm so glad you asked. Many people confuse the two.

The Soul is the spiritual essence of a human being. Often, the term soul is used more or less synonymously with the concept of spirit, although, at least according to some understandings of the soul, this is not correct. The Greek word for soul is psyche. In some contexts, the soul is also defined as active living telepathic contact with a being.[37]

New Me: To me, to put it simply, the mind is my thoughts and feelings, and the soul is my true self. I think it's easy to understand what the body is and, to some extent, the mind, but the soul, that's been difficult. I gradually got better at listening inward instead of listening to all the external sounds and my own thoughts. It's like I have an inner voice that I have to learn to listen to. It's really exciting because my experience is that this is where I find the answers I'm missing, which fit my essence, my soul, or who I really am inside.

Old Me: I think I can sense that I would like to learn something from what you have learnt. Can everyone learn it?

New Me: Yes, everyone can learn it. And remember, you have everything you need. You just need to learn how to train it.

From intelligence to sensory-based learning

There are many commonalities between management theory and learning theory, at least regarding the psychological part. Many years ago, American psychologist and educational researcher Howard Gardner[38] defined seven, and later, two more intelligences, which have since made a valuable contribution to teaching and learning. It's time for this research to be applied to leadership, but we need to adapt it to energetic leadership where senses are dominant.

Historically, *logical-mathematical* intelligence (rational analysis and decision-making) and *linguistic* intelligence (communicating) have been classic leadership virtues, especially in Western cultures, while less emphasis has been placed on others, such as *musical* intelligence (although the term 'orchestration' is often heard in a leadership context) and *spatial* intelligence (which, although it also includes timing, is mainly attributed to product development and creative design).

Gardner's other intelligences include *bodily-kinesthetic* (feeling and mastering one's body – which today is unfortunately often perceived as something to do with ergonomics, leisure activities, or the management team climbing Mount Everest together on the premise that exhaustion is good for the true personalities to emerge), interpersonal (the ability to understand the motivation and co-operation of others), and *intrapersonal* (the ability to form an accurate, truthful picture of oneself and use that picture to perform effectively in life).

Later, Gardner also defined *naturalistic* intelligence (the ability to understand, relate, categorise and explain natural phenomena, including systemic relationships, natural balances and time delays) and existential intelligence (about the intuitive learning element and understanding why we live and why we die).

Through his research, Gardner helps to scientifically underpin that mathematical-logical (decision-making), linguistic (communication) and interpersonal (collaboration) intelligence is not enough to bring out the full potential of either the individual or the organisation. We have so many more intelligences to draw on that just haven't been culturally accommodated in our actions.

The problem with the idea of intelligence is that it doesn't embrace the fluid and intuitive knowledge and wisdom we gather through our senses. As a result, the concept of intelligence becomes incomplete and always lags, and we don't have the full picture to act on. A tangible image of this could be a piece of fabric. If the fabric only consists of intelligence threads one way, it is a flabby piece of fabric (and can't really be called fabric). If the sensory threads are woven in, it becomes a strong piece of fabric.

We need to approach knowledge in a new way where.

1. The needs of the individual come first and affect everything in society
2. We learn when we need to (just-in-time learning)
3. We must learn to use/understand our own energy to solve problems

At the centre of sensory-based learning is the understanding that we make decisions in two different ways based on the impulses we receive:[39]

Traditional decision-making

- *This is the skill we are brought up with and trained in the modern Western world. It is limited, rational, and masculine. The traditional approach is the language and control system of the body and mind.*

Intuitive decision-making

- *The skill we should train to draw on all our wisdom. It is infinite, irrational and feminine. The intuitive approach is the language and operating system of the soul (our soul power).*

Traditional

- Physical behaviour: habit, rules, laws of nature, instinct, mood
- Reason: conviction, data, knowledge, recognition, analysis and arguments
- Emotions: empathy, values, upbringing, role modelling
- Spirit (soul): philosophy, politics, culture, religious beliefs, social code

Intuitive

- Bodily intuition: clairvoyance, signs and clues, synchronicity
- Emotional intuition: clairsentience, mirroring, psychic readings, advice from guides and former relatives
- Mental intuition: claircognisance, clairaudience, common threads in associations, connection to the collective
- Spiritual intuition: clairvoyance, contact with guides, premonitions, dreams and revelations

In the Energetic Leadership Model, they are part of a reinterpretation that is similar but different to Gardner's. Instead of intending that the goal is a level of intelligence, we focus on the learning method by which the intelligence is built. In Energetic Leadership, this involves recognising that the greatest potential lies in using our senses in both traditional and intuitive decision-making:

- The bodily sense: **Feeling** and finding answers in the body through the eight senses (touch, musculoskeletal, balance, sight, hearing, taste, smell), as well as the lesser-known interoception: the sense of feeling physical sensations and knowing what is happening inside the body
- The emotional sense (intrapersonal and interpersonal): **Listening** and thereby helping yourself and others to find answers in harmony with your inner self
- The mental sense: **Looking** behind the emotions and seeking knowledge and insight into the unconscious and your own thoughts and habits
- The intuitive sense: **Believing** and being in touch with your soul

The path to the soul goes through the body, and this is where the bodily sense is essential – it's how we feel. A typical way to explain **bodily sense** is through different professions, such as athletes, dancers, actors, and craftsmen. When football players perform artistry with the world's most sensitive legs and do impossible things, we are witnessing well-developed bodily and kinaesthetic intelligence accumulated through a lifetime of talent and lots of training. They can **feel** their body.

This intelligence is not only traditionally underdeveloped in most of us but is often significantly undervalued as a success factor in modern business management. For many decades, it has been more refined to use one's head, and bodily competencies have been ignored.

But we overlook that the body is our alarm system and our connection to our inner resources. Body awareness is a skill we need to relearn and practise daily. Once we have found the key to feeling our body and shortcut the connection to our autopilot in our brain, we can't help but be present in our body – in a good way, not an unhealthy way. Because it makes us happy. We want to go there again, not back to being out of our own body, as that makes us feel uncomfortable.

The concept of **emotional intelligence** was popularised in 1995 by psychologist Daniel Goleman in the bestseller Emotional Intelligence: Why It Can Matter More Than IQ. At its core is a person's ability to identify and manage their own and others' emotions. This part of our overall sensory system has become significantly more critical as we move from industrialisation into the knowledge and service age because we know, and to some extent accept, that we are energy beings who can listen, manage and use our emotions much more constructively than before.

We have realised the importance of this sense, of being able to **listen** to our emotions and turn it into a vital and useful skill that we can tap into and practise on a daily basis. And when we find the key to hacking our emotional autopilot by reading others and the situation better, thus strengthening our discernment (balancing masculine and feminine energy), life becomes easier and more enjoyable.

Our **mental sense** is the sense with which we "look" and address our thoughts and actions and is stored deeper than our emotions. It is what many people know as the "iceberg" [40]; approximately 5% of our thoughts and emotions are conscious, and approximately 95% are unconscious.

We can benefit greatly from exercising the intuitive mental muscle to get hold of the unconscious part, either by becoming aware of it or by releasing the blocks that the unconscious may contain. We don't need to know everything that gets healed in the process. The most important thing is that we set the intention to receive and sense that thoughts and feelings become lighter. Being able to "see" better by strengthening your mental sense means looking at your habits, adjusting, evaluating, and refining repeatedly. It's knowing the tools available, knowing how to use them and recognising what works.

The **intuitive sense** enables us to reach the next level of understanding by **believing** what we **sense** (feel), **hear** (listen), and **see** (look). To be in touch with our body, and to know and understand our thoughts, feelings, and behaviour patterns. It's a bit like needing to have the key to the three doors in the escape room before you can enter the innermost room and be in touch with your intuition – your soul.

At first, you may have to choose to believe – to go with your gut feeling because it's unfamiliar to you, and you lack the experience to know for sure that it works. Later, as you become more consciously aware, you will trust your intuition more. Your intuition sends you signals all the time, which you learn to pick up with your transmitting and receiver mast (you and your body) through your senses.

The training of and with our energy is so transformative that change happens at the cellular level, where cells are "re-coded". One habit at a time. One belief/skill at a time.

The training takes place in all kinds of everyday situations and less common situations. In any situation where something is happening around you, tempting you or influencing you from the outside, you are right at the crossroads (see the figure below, where the downward and upward curves intersect). For example, you're offered a piece of chocolate, a frustrated colleague asks for your help, or you have to consider an assignment and decide within 30 minutes whether you want to accept it or not.

At that moment, you receive impulses from outside and inside. You have to decide whether you want to go up or down in the energetic leadership of the situation at hand, i.e. you breathe, turn your gaze inwards briefly, tap into the situation with all your senses, find the balance and then decide what is best – in other words, you go up in your energetic leadership. Or do you go down because you have put your energy tools aside and make a quick autopilot decision with your head, which may seem easy and effective within that moment, but not in the long run, neither for yourself nor for others involved, because it was unbalanced at the moment of decision.

Developing your sensory ability and energetic (self-)leadership is about unlearning and relearning habits and beliefs. Our cells are intense energy factories, and learning generates energy. Learning is also infinite. Both unlearning (the downward curve) and (re)learning (the upward curve) happen throughout life.

It has become more and more legitimate to talk about stress and breakdown as more and more people experience stress or other illnesses at some point in their lives. In particular, many highly intuitive, sensory adept, truthful people have suffered. They are suffering (we see it even more so in the younger generation[41]) in this very unintuitive world, which is built with the best of intentions from huge amounts of data and knowledge in structures, boxes, systems, processes, and business models that are very fixed and linear. It's not easy having to constantly silence the inner voice screaming that there's no sense in the madness or that there's something much more important than what we're doing right now.

Fortunately, it seems the world – with a portion of consciously aware adults and an even larger portion of young people up to age 35 – is now ready to take a stand and expect recognition of the knowledge we receive through all four senses. They appreciate that this is how we create complete individuals and that it is the symbiosis between the actional and the intuitive that we need to live by to be sustainable in the inner first and then the outer.

Energy and consciousness

"We are from the Stars but of the Earth."[42] Science is researching human beings as energy with frequency, and increasingly, ordinary people are also starting to take an interest in it – both scientifically and personally. A new movement of energy awareness is rolling across the world like a much-needed helping hand. This heightened awareness of man's energetic role in the universe is the foundation of the new age.

Some organisations have already understood it – seen the light – and are promoting the need for agile organisations with a high organisational heartbeat that is flexible and value-based.

If you're a manager feeling sceptical, please read the introduction and the nine trends in chapter 2 again, keeping in mind that irritation is your key to change. Your employees are already largely influenced by this increased awareness and are acting on it.

It is the new awareness that everything is energy and everything/ everybody is connected that can and will help us understand our challenges and the solutions that may exist. There is potential for greater awareness of how we think, where our thoughts stem from, and what knowledge is actually hidden in our bodies when almost 95% of it is unconscious and unrealised. What a gift and opportunity the future holds – this is truly the century of possibilities.

When we learn to work with our energy, we get to the bottom of our unconscious mind. We can remove the blocks ourselves by sensing our body through energy. By "cleansing" the innermost part of ourselves, we gain better access to and focus on our intention. This can connect us with our cause and our passion, which is often either neglected or unconsciously fighting against the reality we are a part of.

In this way, we tap into everything that is also a part of us, that lies at the bottom – a bit like finding a treasure trove of magical, sparkling diamonds and pearls. We think and feel with our entire body. We don't just think with our heads. And we can act in harmony with who we are. We can create and co-create. Physically, the frequency in the body will be higher, and thus, we generate more energy ourselves. We can create a positive upward spiral of development for ourselves and each other. On the other hand, if we are unbalanced, the frequency will be low and provide less energy, making us less resilient, and we may end up getting sick.

Unfortunately, right now, many people and organisations are suffering from constipation and pent-up energy. Suppose we recognise that we are energy and that we are connected with a new awareness and understanding. In that case, we are on our way to getting to the bottom of people's fundamental traits, flaws, physical imbalances, and the unhappiness and inefficiencies of organisations. In doing so, we can unlock the energy and potential needed to find new solutions to create a better balance in the world for the benefit of everyone and the planet.

Although it may feel foreign to some, we can easily learn to understand and practise this energy awareness. It's a skill – and we've had it before, but we've forgotten to use the muscle. It's the most essential skill of the past and the most vital skill of the future, so let's dive even deeper into what an energetic person is.

Ellen Meredith, a recognised energy educator, calls energy a language (a source language, our first language). We are able to receive messages from the body, mind and soul by using movement, light, sound, vibration, images, actions, interaction with energy flows, and their presence in the environment.

Future medicine will be the medicine of frequencies"

- Einstein

While we can cure and prevent many diseases by living at high frequencies, the language of energy is not just a language we need to master when we are sick or want to prevent illness. It is our natural, innate language that we should be able to master in everyday life to balance our own masculine and feminine energies, draw in the energy we need, and especially understand when something or a situation requires our special conscious attention and navigate it. We must relearn how to master this invisible language, our first language.

Our task will thus be:

- to build a capacity for perceiving subtle energies
- to learn the tools of subtle perception
- to develop and communicate with subtle energies
- to live and lead naturally from subtle energy awareness

Working with your energy is often referred to as energy work. It means increasing frequency by doing less and doing the right and important things in a balanced way. It's about conscious self-care and, in essence, charity. When we "tidy up" in ourselves (personal development), we also help those around us in our private lives, at work and in the world. The energy becomes cleaner and uplifting.

It's about healing our mind and the traumas we all carry, big and small, that have consequences for our body and well-being, translating into unhealthy behaviour and relationships. An unhealthy wheel of malaise that has roots down to the cellular level, inherited through generations.

We can heal the body, mind and soul when all three are one and unite in symbiosis. We do this by calibrating the energy in the body, bringing the right and left sides together. We do this by reprogramming ourselves from being a low-frequency transmitter and receiver mast to a high-frequency transmitter and receiver mast by setting and using intention to direct the energy to areas of the body that "crunch" physically and/or emotionally and massage the area. By setting the intention and letting the energy and our focus and awareness do the work, we can tap into the deepest darkness and remove the leading causes of discomfort and/or failure to realise our full potential.

Thanks to quantum physics and its sensitive measuring devices, energy can now be measured. All our energy centres can be measured and recorded. Even though we're already moving away from using only our brains to gain insights and understand connections, it helps many to realise that there is science behind this madness.

Did you know that the body's physical, measurable voltage levels (the pressure from a circuit's power source that enables it to perform a task, like lighting a light bulb or firing up the grey matter) change with our health and activity?[43]

- Sick body: 5-9 mV
- Healthy body: 30-100 mV
- Top athletes doing meditation, Qigong or Tai Chi: 2000 mV

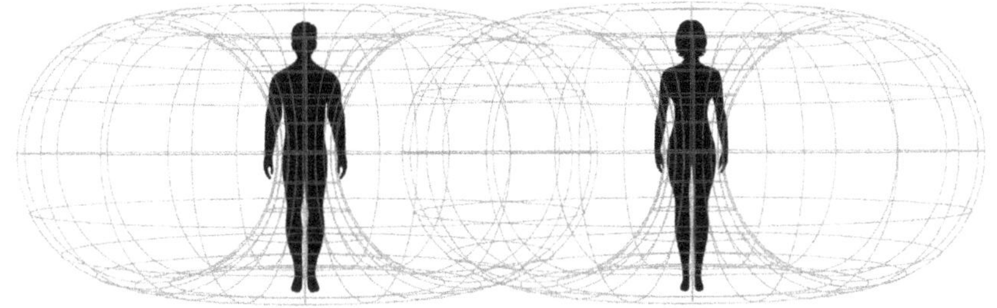

If there's one thing that elite athletes are better at than the rest of us, it's disciplined training. Remarkably, their voltage is 20-60 times higher when they practise QiGong, Tai Chi and meditation than an average healthy body. And now it's getting a bit technical, but hang on because the point is super interesting! Just as you can change the speed of a motor by changing the frequency (number of oscillations per second) of the voltage that drives the motor, you can also change the "speed" and performance of your body by changing the frequency.

Exercising (in general, not just the types of exercise mentioned above) increases the frequency and, therefore, voltage levels. The great thing about these gentle forms of exercise is that they also provide the opportunity to expand consciousness by resetting over and over again. This can be done in different forms and in other monotonous activities such as weeding or walking alone in nature. The intention is to do "consciousness yoga", where you expand and stretch energy by being fully present – to reset – and then practising daily to be better and better at sensing what is happening in your inner life.

Initially, this often requires a special setting, but we gradually learn to be able to do it in real life, at work, in public or at home. Eventually, energy work can become like driving a car, much of which happens unconsciously yet with a focused awareness of the conditions.

Introverts have an advantage in the future in that they thrive and gather energy in their own company and naturally try to create the breaks they need either consciously or by withdrawing, unlike extroverts, who gain energy in the company of others and can find it almost frightening when it's quiet and empty. The future is the age of the introvert, and we see it when a top executive, such as the CEO of pharmaceutical company Novo Nordisk, Lars Fruergaard Jørgensen, publicly talks about how he deals with being an introverted top executive, needing breaks in his agenda.

It is the contact with the soul that makes working with energy easier and better, and life becomes a flow, a form of enjoyment where we experience being strong in our own inner core, both physically, mentally and spiritually. This is where intuition becomes self-driving and is set free. Everything feels right. It's like when a stiff and locked body becomes as soft as butter after combining physical, mental and spiritual training.

Stress, which is low frequency, shuts down energy. It's a self-perpetuating negative process. So the energy needs to be maintained. There is some inner fuel that needs to be created. Some "energy-conscious yoga" needs to be done. We need to learn how to increase our energy – how to become agile in our energy, just like we do flexibility exercises.

To better understand ourselves, it's good to know our energy centres. Hindus recognise a number of energy centres, most commonly grouped into six chakras (meaning 'wheel' in Sanskrit). They are governed by the seventh and uppermost chakra on the isthmus, Sahasrara (meaning the lotus with a thousand petals).[44] [45]

The chakras (energy centres) are located along the spine. In the visual representations, each chakra has its colour, and each colour has a distinct meaning. The chakras are connected to your thoughts, feelings and habits. If your emotions or lifestyle are imbalanced, your chakras will also become imbalanced.

When we have imbalances, it manifests as unhappiness or outright illness. Chakras with good flow without clots are like veins and arteries without clots. We readily appreciate that we need to avoid calcifications so that blood can flow freely and joyfully in our body. The same applies to our energy through the 7 "control" chakra points.

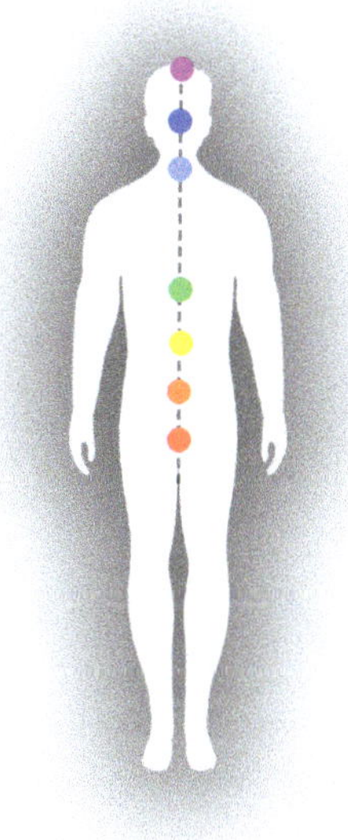

The seven chakras also have different frequencies, with each chakra connected to an organ or gland to which they regulate energy. Our "new" skill is to influence the frequencies so that the chakras come into balance and release the blocked energy[46] [47]:

Chakra (energy centres)	Function	Solfeggio tone and frequency*	Benefit
Red -Root, the spine	Creates grounding to the energy and alignment to the body	UT 396 Hz	Releases guilt, shame and fear and creates a foundation for trust, joy and safety
Orange - Hara, diaphragm below the navel	Stimulates sexuality and emotions, increasing fertility, creativity and willingness to share emotions	RE 417 Hz	Recognises and forgives situations and facilitates change that brings a zest for life, enjoyment and connection to the inner child
Yellow – Solar plexus, abdomen	Stimulates will and vitality (centre of emotions).	MI 528 Hz	Transforms and creates miracles through the feeling of life mastery, increasing power and gratitude
Green – Heart	Creates a connection between the physical and spiritual world	FA 639 Hz	Connects and creates relationships through empathy, compassion, unconditional love, acceptance, trust, forgiveness and peace
Light blue – Throat	Opens up energetic and spiritual communication by connecting body and mind	SOL 741 Hz	Awakens intuition through creativity
Blue – 3rd eye between the two eyes	Connects to universal unconsciousness and increases intuition and integrity by being able to see within	LA 852 Hz	Consciously opens the 3rd eye to see the world in a whole new light
Purple – Top of the head	Brings about deeper consciousness and creates a deeper energetic understanding of the spiritual	TI 963 Hz	Balance and a good sense of direction in life, seeing the path as light. Inner stillness, lightness of mind and strong intuition.

heals and balances the chakras with its sounds and tones

There is infinite energy available in the universe. There's no need to let the old fears and competitive mentality drive you to hold on to knowledge and sensations. The energy reveals our condition anyway. There is enough energy for everyone. You receive the energy healing you are ready to receive according to your level of consciousness. In this way, understanding energy and working with (increasing and managing) your energy and resources becomes a competency built on trust.

And when we have this competence, we feel better about ourselves. We have better relationships. We feel better in our personal and professional lives. We become better leaders. It becomes easier to be and contribute to the community at work and the surrounding society.

Intuition as a superpower

Energy is our raw material, and as described above, we can increase our frequency and energy through awareness work. It is the energy that feeds our intuition, which is the vital "new" competency of the future.

Intuition allows us to draw on all our inner resources and believe in the wisdom we possess in our innermost being. It is what allows us to be and act authentically and in harmony with our true life purpose. As such, intuition is the prerequisite for our mental and spiritual health and for us to interact optimally with the world around us. It is the key to our true potential.

Some sources, such as the Cambridge Dictionary, define intuition as "an ability to understand or know something without needing to think about it or use reason to discover it, or a feeling that shows this ability". In other words, it's disconnected from the head.

Pauline Skov Poulsen , who educates people in intuition,[48] defines it as "the ability to let oneself be guided through life using one's biological receiving and transmitting capacity to reach goals and unfold its potential over time with greater learning and deepest joy".

The last definition is more apt. We are a receiving and sending transmitter mast. We receive signals without doing anything. However, we need to learn to be good receivers because we tend to ignore signals if they don't align with what we expect, or the message is too uncomfortable or challenges our comfort level. In this context, it is worth noting that we find a sense of safety in the familiar – even if it's both uncomfortable and unhealthy.

It's important to emphasise that we always receive the signals. They are stored in our subconscious – in the unconscious 95%, if not in the conscious part. We need to practise receiving signals more consciously, process them, and use the special wisdom they contain so that they become part of our conscious thought processes.

This is exactly what Einstein refers to when he says, "The intuitive mind is a sacred gift, and the rational mind is a faithful servant". We have come to earth with a huge bang and turned everything upside down. Our task is to find our sacred gift, our soul, through our intuition. Then, we need to use our 'faithful servant' – our head – our rational mind and our ego to support us.

Pauline Skov Poulsen also says: "Energy is the raw material of intuition and a transmitter of messages. We need to ensure that there is enough energy for the body, senses, nervous system and brain to communicate optimally with each other. In this way, our physique is a signalling system through which intuition communicates, and energy is the connector in intuitive communication internally and externally. The total amount of energy varies from person to person, but we can optimise energy by being aware of how we use it physically, emotionally, mentally, and spiritually" [49].

The better the energy, the better the intuition, the better the awareness. I could add: The better the awareness, the better the intuition, the more energy. You could go as far as to say that recognising the role of intuition has an impact on our ability to innovate. The more in touch with our intuition, the more creative we become. Intuition helps us draw not only from the conscious mind but also from the vast ocean of wisdom and creativity that we are unconscious of.

The superpower of intuition is super-charged when we switch on intention and obtain rocket fuel. The intuitive person who sets the intention to achieve what they set out to do and is persistent with their passion will go far in an easy and enjoyable way.

In professional leadership, energy awareness and energy management will be both an age-old discipline but also a brand new and unavoidable aspect of management, soon to be the talk of the town. Leaders who choose the buzzword route can expect resistance from workers (overt or quiet resignation). It can't be repeated too often; this new awareness of inner sustainability and energy is already in full bloom in many organisations, albeit somewhat invisible to management.

Energetic leadership doesn't seem to fit neatly into the age-old, traditional masculine dominance because it's not something that can be easily fixed and done or managed the old-fashioned way. Nor can it be delegated to others. Our frequency reveals us, and the only way forward is to be energetically balanced and understand its depth and implications. Yourself! You need to develop a language and a personal practice around it.

High and good energy creates good flow, and the opposite creates clogged energy in people, relationships, and collaborations. Clogged energy hinders intuition and reduces awareness.

Einstein, our good friend, said a long time ago that the remedy is to change the frequency. Not to stuff yourself with conventional medicine to numb the symptoms or accept a mediocre, unsatisfying, unfulfilled life and career. It makes us sick. We are creating a poor world around us. The conscious and skilled employees don't want to take part in that anymore.

In the organisation, the management team can work to increase energy, awareness and intuition by asking themselves the following questions:

- Have there been resignations that could indicate that the company is also affected by the great resignation?
- Is it possible that there is quiet resignation in the company?
- What does management believe about the company's level of energy, intuition and awareness?

- Does management's attitude have a positive or negative impact on the future of the organisation?
- Does management ask the organisation about these issues? (perhaps the organisation is more advanced in terms of awareness than management)

Working with energy, intuition, and awareness is relevant to personal leadership in all roles. Everyone needs to bring their physical, mental, and spiritual competencies into play, and this will be the greatest gift to the person and the company.

You can work with your energy, intuition and consciousness in the following ways:

1. Commit to being fully present (set the intention)
2. Lean into receiving the gift (silence) and let go of the noise in your energy before you start.
3. Calm down with minus breathing (exercise 5 in the back of the book)
4. Reach your senses with resetting (exercise 3 in the back of the book)
5. Be still and listen to your body (exercise 1 in the back of the book

At the back of the book, you will find a series of exercises that will help you get into the right state and maximise the benefits.

The exercises help you to be at peace in your soul energy – in contact with your soul.

Ask the following questions:

- From where does your body "speak" to you? Where in your body do you feel something?
- What is the feeling of the place in your body that "speaks"?
- What colour (if you see colours) is the place in your body that "speaks"?
- What sound does the place in your body that "speaks" make
  - Intuitively switch on the sound
  - See what sound comes out of your mouth
  - Keep saying the sound until it becomes more harmonious
- What does your "talking" body want to tell you?

Make a daily note of what energises you, what your energy is like and what affects it. This will help you get to know it better.

Chakra calibration is a great way to align energy centres and energetically merge the left and right sides of the body. It can be done from top to bottom and in the following way:

☐ Do points 1-5 (above) so that you are calm and focused.

☐ Take a deep breath and start from the head chakra by making tiny circular movements with your inner gaze down through the energy centres of the spine. Don't rush the process, but take the time your body needs. Notice where the body has a harder time passing an energy centre, where there is an 'energy crunch'. This is where the body "talks" to you.

☐ When you have reached all the way down to the root chakra (tailbone), anchor the energy into the ground by saying in your mind that you are doing this. It is your intention, focus and presence that guides your energy.

We are in the midst of a great and wild, energetic revolution. Since the concept of energy is so new to all of us, it might be a good idea to have some simple principles to live by.

The 5 energetic principles could be:

1. Set the pace of the day according to your energy
2. Reset your energy several times a day
3. Train your energy awareness daily
4. Ask and let your intuition guide you
5. Be grateful

As a leader, it's worth remembering the different characteristics of the generations and that there are differences in how quickly different parts of the workforce and different types of people adopt new ideas and thoughts.

Also, keep in mind that this is a pervasive, fast-moving trend that doesn't fail to affect our employees because we are personally sceptical. It's pretty certain that large parts of the workforce are already well on their way to this awareness. We see it in the *great resignation*, and we see it in the materialism vs. spirituality curve; for the new generations, energy work is natural and is expected to be part of how they work.

The nervous system

The nervous system is essential to our ability to manage ourselves better, each other and our planet. When we want to make changes in our outer world, we need to include the inner world. That's why it's important to understand how we physiologically function as humans. When the nervous system isn't working, we can't hear our body, we can't produce energy, we can't function at all.

The nervous system isn't just in one place; it's all over the body. It is affected by basic things like sleeping, eating, and exercising. However, many other things also affect our body, mind and soul through our nervous system.

The nervous system consists of two parts: the sympathetic and para-sympathetic nervous systems.

In simple terms, the **sympathetic** nervous system enables the body to react quickly and purposefully to danger. It is a fight and flight action that is triggered when we recognise that something is happening, for example, if a tiger were about to attack or we were about to crash the car.

The **parasympathetic** nervous system enables the body to normalise the situation. So when the danger is over, i.e. the tiger is gone, or the car is righted, a reaction of calm and rest occurs, which is necessary to rebuild the body.

If we want to thrive and avoid living in a constantly stressed situation, then we can't expose the sympathetic nervous system, the fight-flight system, to danger all the time. It's something the body can handle when it happens once in a while, but not all the time. And it's not only in life-threatening situations that our sympathetic nervous system is activated. It is also activated when you encounter an angry colleague, boss or customer who is angry at you or you realise you've made a huge mistake and sent an email to the wrong recipient.

Unfortunately, with our modern way of living and leading, we live in fear – fear that we inherit from our kin and fear that is part of our culture, upbringing, and systems and that is embedded in our cells and behaviour. When combined with stress, fear is a bad cocktail for the person and their environment. Our nervous system is then in a more or less constant fight-or-flight state and not in a balanced, calm position. And often, this happens without us realising it.

When we are in fight-or-flight mode, the soul leaves the body because it can't cope with being there. It shuts down because it's not a nice place to live in a stressed body. And that's actually okay if it's just for a brief remark that the soul says okay, now you're about to crash, so I'll look after you by not being present. But it's not okay when it happens often or even becomes permanent.

For the past 500 years, modern humans have been struggling to create growth, being extremely busy, and allowing ourselves to be controlled too much by our masculine energy. As a result, we have lost touch with what actually makes sense to us. Our inner self is screaming that the world is broken and that we need to do something different than we usually do. But we can't hear it. Our body is important because it is the mouthpiece of the soul. It's important that we can hear what our body is saying and, through it, can access the 95% of our consciousness that is unconscious. When the soul leaves our body, we are not in touch with ourselves.

The immune system is a snitch. It is an army of tiny soldiers that go to battle when we are exposed to bacteria, viruses and other disease-causing organisms. Without the body's natural healing army, we wouldn't survive, but when the immune system works as it should, we don't notice it. The immune system can be measured using a blood test, which includes looking for white blood cells called leukocytes. These are important for the immune system and come in different subtypes.

When there is an imbalance in the body, it leads to deficiencies and diseases. First, the deficiencies raise their voice to grab our attention, then the diseases, and finally the miserable quality of life or death. You might wonder why we choose the path of not listening because the consequences of that choice are obvious.

We need to regain body awareness so that we can start problem-solving where the problem originated. We need to get back in balance with ourselves so we can hear and feel our bodies. And so that we can hear and feel our mind, eliminating racing and disturbing thoughts and instead letting our thoughts drift away by simply observing them. The nervous system is essential in this process.

While it's quite marvellous what the body can do, our shell is relatively slow to rebuild itself. It takes three months to create new neural pathways and 35 days to restore the epidermis.

Our minds are faster. We have 60-80,000 thoughts a day. A good portion of them are repetitive and negative – and the vast majority are executed on autopilot.

But the most important thing to remember is that the soul is as fast as lightning, slipping away if we lack awareness and don't give it space to play a role. If there's too much fear and racing thoughts in a stressed, inflamed body, the soul is gone, and we're left to steer our ship with a rudderless body, which is very difficult. We work and work and work and can't understand why we don't get more out of our efforts. However, when body, mind and soul are aligned, life and work become much more fun and easier. It becomes, as the saying goes, "smarter, not harder".

The body is slow
The mind is fast
The soul is lightning fast (in disappearing)

Sleep

Sleep is fundamental for all of us. We spend about a third of the day sleeping. And at the same time, we have a frightening number of challenges with it.[50]

Various studies worldwide have shown the prevalence of insomnia in 10%–30% of the population, some even as high as 50%–60%. Both the acute and chronic forms of insomnia are very common. Roughly 1 in 3 adults worldwide have insomnia symptoms, and about 10% of adults meet the criteria for insomnia disorder.

That's a shame because sleep is both wonderful and something our body needs. We digest and re-energise. We dream and store knowledge in long-term memory.

Sleep affects our nervous system, physique, and mood. It is possibly the most crucial factor in determining the way we are present in our lives, our performance, our physical health, and our mental state. It's our soul's best friend because, without sleep, the hero is no good at all.

So, as a leader in an organisation, you're interested in being well rested yourself – and your organisation. This can be difficult to navigate because sleep is also a very private matter. It happens at home outside of working hours. But it's just so crucial to how an organisation thrives and what actually underlies any malaise or lack of results that we need to overcome this barrier.

So how can you, as a leader, initiate dialogue with employees about their sleep situation? An obvious question to ask in conversations with employees where you have a feeling that there is stress or something else going on could simply be: How do you sleep at night?

We can be professional at work, respect privacy, and at the same time have a culture of openness about life's challenges. And maybe the answer is "harmless" if, for example, the baby isn't sleeping, and we can talk openly about strategies for "survival" during that period. Or maybe the person finally opens the floodgates and tells us about their unhappiness in the department, and we can strategise to change the culture, change the tasks or something else entirely.

We need to stop ignoring the signals we receive and trust that we all have a common interest in healthy nervous systems and that it's okay to talk about your discomfort without risking a professional backslide, jeopardising your career. As leaders, we need to insist that openness and asking for help is a sign of a solid self-management capability, not the opposite.

Another way to show understanding and be helpful in a concrete way is to have a quiet room in the company where you can go and just sit down, collect yourself, and recharge your batteries. This will benefit not only those who are tired but also introverts who feel worn out by a noisy or crowded open-plan environment.

Perhaps there could even be an opportunity to lie down for half an hour? Perhaps it could be combined with a space for meditation, stretching, or the opportunity to practise your religion?

And personally, in your own leadership, it is, of course, also important to focus on your sleep and sleep habits. There are so many tools nowadays that can measure both the quantity and quality of sleep. If you have sleep issues, it can be a good idea to use gadgets to gain knowledge and insight that you can't argue with. It can be the starting point for doing something about it.

Others live without technological aids, listening to their body and observing the signals – without relying on data. Because we know. We know if we lack energy during the day. We just don't listen, or we misinterpret the signal because the truth is uncomfortable, and change requires us to look at ourselves and the choices we should be making. But that's precisely what we must do: Notice, listen and see. And trust that our soul is telling us what we need.

As a minimum, you should ask yourself these questions:

- Do you care about your sleep?
- How do you spend your time? Are you sleeping long enough?
- Do you have good sleep hygiene and good sleep habits?
- Is the room at the right temperature?
- Is the bed good?

- Is the bedroom mobile-free?
- Do you have a wind-down routine before you go to sleep – or do you eat, smoke, exercise, drink and watch TV/mobile just before you go to sleep?

Some tips for optimising or improving sleep can be:

☐ Note any challenges you may have in a sleep log and follow up on whether you are experiencing the desired improvements you have set out to achieve.

☐ Notice if you are looking forward to sleep or if you are not looking forward to sleep.

☐ Take it seriously if you don't wake up feeling refreshed even after sleeping. See a doctor for an assessment of the problem, as this is not normal.

☐ Avoid eating after 8 pm.

☐ Avoid doing a lot of exercise right before you go to sleep unless it's sex :-)

☐ Have a slow-down routine so your body gets used to a different pace and looks forward to sleeping.

☐ No screens in the last hour(s) before bedtime.

☐ Use meditation or sound healing as an enjoyment ritual before going to sleep (exercises 7 and 8 in the back of the book).

☐ Pray before you go to sleep. Not that there is necessarily anything religious about it, but be grateful for what has happened during the day (exercise 2 in the back of the book).

☐ Send your intentions for the next day at the same time, so you have peace of mind about what's going to happen (exercise 2 in the back of the book).

☐ Use a sleep mask so that it's always completely dark and your brain can calm down. A thick or heavy duvet can also help the body to calm down.

The fact that one in three adults worldwide have sleep issues suggests that many don't take them seriously. In fact, poor sleep is, at best, unhelpful in the short term but fatal in the long term. We simply die earlier if we don't give our body and nervous system the rest they need – especially if we already have other illnesses like diabetes.[51] [52]

Food

It comes as no surprise that eating and drinking are absolutely fundamental to us. But most people overlook the fact that it's not just about hunger, thirst, and physical well-being.

We eat something solid; we take in some fluids. It can be healthy; it can be unhealthy. It can be local. It can be made somewhere else. It can be blandly presented or beautifully presented. It can be varied, and it can be monotonous. It can be tasty, and it can be unpalatable. It can be quick to make, or it can be very time-consuming. It could be that we eat out of necessity. We may also be comfort eating.

Our food and eating habits can be traditional or non-traditional. Some eat everything, including meat. Others eat plant-based, vegan, vegetarian, Ayurvedic, or something else. Throughout time, traditions and attitudes towards food constantly change regarding what is healthy, sensible, and trendy, as well as what we bother to prepare and how much time we spend cooking and eating the meal.

What is abundantly clear is that despite many years of national dietary guidelines (which far from everyone agrees on), we have a lot of analysed results showing that we are becoming more and more overweight.[53]

Worldwide obesity has tripled since 1975, according to WHO. In 2016, more than 1.9 billion adults, 18 years and older, were overweight. Of these, over 650 million were obese. And the figures are developing in the wrong direction.

We find it difficult to eat healthily. We are getting sicker and sicker with illnesses like allergies, diabetes, osteoarthritis, cancer, and high blood pressure as the most common conditions. The occurrence of individual diseases and health problems has increased with foresight modelling indicating that 60% of adult men, 50% of adult women and about 25% of all children under 16 could be obese by 2050. There are plenty of signs that we're not living healthily, although it's hardly due to a lack of knowledge.

Food is essential for us to function physically – we all know that. But in fact, what we eat and how we eat it also has a big impact on our sociability and our senses. It matters that we take the time to prepare our food, arrange it nicely, eat it with people we enjoy being with and eat it slowly so that we experience the flavours that aid digestion.

The entire meal staging affects our senses, thus our nervous system and digestion. Interestingly, when we start eating healthier, it affects our physical, mental, and spiritual well-being and can start a positive spiral. Better food produces better blood glucose control, which sparks an appetite for better food, which increases energy, etc.

The five official dietary guidelines from the WHO are beneficial to follow – and they are good for both your personal health and the climate:

1. Breastfeed babies and young children
2. Eat a variety of foods
3. Eat plenty of vegetables and fruits
4. Eat moderately of fats and oils
5. Eat less salts and sugars

You can do it cheaper, easier and better by following these two tips:

- Minimise food waste for you and the planet
- Look for the official Keyhole label when you shop, though it is only available in the Nordic countries (the EU and other countries find that kind of labelling too complicated to establish). This makes it easier to cut down on fat, sugar, and salt and get more fibre and whole grains.[54]

But you can also be more ambitious and increase your awareness of your body's condition by going all-in and testing whether some of the other trends work for you. Give it a few months and practise every day to feel the difference. Let's look at a few of them.

The Alkaline Institute recommends eating according to the **acid-base balance**, which is basically about eating a balanced diet in which at least 70-80% of what we consume is base-forming. The postulate is that acid-forming food creates a long-term breeding ground for bad bacteria and fungi because they thrive in the low-oxygen environment it creates.

The first signs of an acidic body are tiredness and weight problems. Acid builds up in your tissues to protect your organs, but if your diet contains too much acid and too little base, an inflammatory state is created. You will feel pain either in your joints or muscles, and you will experience irritation and fatigue. Eventually, this can lead to weight gain, diabetes, allergies, skin problems, and other symptoms.[55] [56]

You can add more alkaline to your diet by eating more vegetables and fibre and by avoiding meat, dairy, eggs, cheese, sugar and alcohol, coffee and black tea.

Eating and living **Ayurvedically** is also gaining ground. In Ayurveda, it is claimed that "your food is your medicine". Ayurveda means "science of life" in Sanskrit and is based on ancient Vedic scriptures. Ayurveda is a system that is more than 5,000 years old, making it the world's oldest health science for a long, healthy, and happy life in balance with the elements, seasons, and cycles of nature [57]. Ayurveda is thus the science of our entire life for body, mind, and soul – even how we should build our houses.

In Ayurvedic diet, food is categorised as heavy/light, dry/liquid and hot/cold. There are six 'flavours' (sweet, sour, salty, bitter, astringent and pungent). A balanced meal should contain food from all categories to balance the different doshas.

The doshas are composed of the five elements of nature and have the properties of the elements: ether, air, fire, water and earth. Inside the body, these elements are combined into three life forces or doshas: Vata (space and air), Pitta (water and fire) and Kapha (water and earth). In Ayurveda, it is believed that everyone is born with a unique combination of these three doshas, but there is always one dosha that is more prominent in the body than others.

* * *

As a company, you can easily do something to promote a healthy food culture. This can be done through what is served in the canteen, but also through the traditions and habits you have around food and drink. In addition, the company's contribution to food waste, energy consumption and waste management.

- How does the company's food culture relate to its mission, principles, values and brand?
- Does the company have a healthy food culture in the canteen and around meetings?
- Are employees involved in developing the food culture?
- Does the company have an open culture about talking about food, weight and well-being?
- Does the company fulfil sustainability goals related to food waste, energy consumption and waste management?

In your personal leadership, you can look at your own dietary habits, and one question in particular comes to mind: Why?

- What is the reason that you eat unhealthy food? Is it loneliness, sadness, anger, lack of sleep, stress?
- When do you eat unhealthy food?

Be honest with yourself. Only when you have identified the underlying causes do you have a real opportunity to adjust your diet and reprogram your life.

☐ Read the dietary guidelines and check if you are following them. Write down which ones you want to follow to a larger extent.

☐ Every time you eat or drink something, note whether you do it out of hunger, anger, loneliness or fatigue, and what thoughts and feelings you have before and after you eat or snack.

☐ Make a note of what you eat and what illnesses and ailments you have – and note which ones you want to get rid of first and what you think it will take.

Start by focusing on changing one habit that can affect your health, such as drinking enough water. And when that habit sticks, change the next habit. Focus your attention on the positive effect – feel what it does for you in body and mind – and bring the pleasure right into your soul. Teach your body to recognise what it needs and what enjoyment is for you. Stable blood sugar levels are essential for both mood and health.[58] [59] [60]

Be patient and smile to yourself at your progress.

Exercise

We all have some sort of relationship with exercise. And most of us think of it as something physical. We love walking and running, swimming, rowing, playing ball and something with a racket or a horse. We have good habits, and we have bad habits. We enjoy it, we think it's hard, it provides us with a community, and we set lots of New Year's resolutions – and struggle to keep them.

Exercise helps to keep our casing going and our immune response strong, and it also helps to keep our nervous system healthy. It strengthens our muscles and tendons and improves breathing, circulation and digestion. Because when we exercise our muscles, our bodies become better at doing what we ask of them. The muscles become better at absorbing oxygen because they have more small blood vessels, and the energy depots in the muscles are developed to be better equipped to burn fat and store carbohydrates (sugar). In addition, we get lots of lovely feel-good hormones, also known as endorphins. A good measure of our condition is the flexibility of the spine.

However, in this section, exercise also includes mental and spiritual exercise. When we feel better physically in our body, we are also more likely to feel better mentally. We better connect with our Soul when physical and mental challenges are not interfering.

We can exercise our thoughts and spirituality, just as we can exercise our bodies physically. Most people know this, but many may not know how to do it. And it may not be socially accepted in all contexts.

We need to get better at recognising that exercise is also inner-directed maintenance and not just about how we look on the outside. We are thinking and feeling beings, and we need to get better at taking care of and exercising our physical, mental and spiritual powers. Self-care is not only about physicality but also about being able to speak up and be still. You can sit or lie down, or you can enjoy a bath or be in nature, which is a very healing place.

Physical exercise could be:

- **Strength training:** Strengthening muscles and tendons, e.g. through classic gymnastics and fitness exercises or swimming
- **Cardio training**: Strengthen circulation, e.g. by brisk walking, running and cycling
- **Flexibility training**: Strengthen the eyes, connective tissue, and musculoskeletal system, e.g., with yin yoga exercises and eye exercises to reduce stiffness after screens[61].

You can easily combine the three. Going for a brisk walk and looking up also strengthens the eyes and helps transport knowledge to long-term memory so we know how to do things and understand what people are saying. Make a pit stop on your walk to do a plank exercise, hoist yourself into a tree, and sit and stare out at the sea for a while. Then you'll be well on your way.

Exercising the *mental* could be:

- Doing breathing exercises
- Being with others
- Being and walking in nature
- Dancing
- Taking a cold bath or dip in the winter sea
- Speaking nicely to yourself
- Being loving to yourself and others

To exercise the *soulful* could be:

- Silent listening (exercise 1 in the back of the book)
- Meditating (exercise 7 in the back of the book)
- Listening to light language (exercise 8 in the back of the book)
- Listening to music with healing frequencies
- Walking barefoot on the grass or ground
- Being true to yourself

In many organisations, exercise is part of the staff policy and culture. But in many of them, there's little focus on what exercise actually is. That it is physical, mental and spiritual.

Companies can contribute to developing an energy-conscious organisation by:

- ☐ Relating exercise to community, freedom, and leadership, as it helps the individual and the community to function from their true core.

☐ Including physical, mental and spiritual exercise in cultural work and people policy.

☐ Taking the lead in leadership and use, e.g., exercise and nature as part of meetings and conversations.

In the leadership of people, you should also ensure physical, mental and spiritual exercise.

- How can I make **physical** exercise a natural part of my work and life based on the philosophy that everything counts and adds up?
  - Walk as much as possible, take breaks and do stretching exercises with your arms against the wall
  - Use the sit-stand desk
  - Do eye exercises every hour – look away from the screen and out into the horizon
- How can I practise **mental** training throughout the day to build a healthy habit?
  - Stay in your own lane – concentrate on what concerns you and your tasks.
  - Say thank you or help a colleague.
  - Breathe if a thought has run wild and become judgemental.
- Make room for **spiritual** exercise in your everyday life:
  - Use a quiet room or the outdoors to sit quietly and listen with your eyes closed for 5-10 minutes.
  - Stand firm on what you feel – and say no and thank you.
  - Be grateful and recognise the positive in everyone and the situation.

Thoughts, feelings and beliefs

As mentioned, we have 60-80,000 thoughts a day. These are thoughts that come and go and that we don't necessarily relate to. In fact, we only actively engage with very few of them.

Thoughts and feelings can be nice, and they can be bad. You can be sad or happy. The mind doesn't know what time it is, and thoughts can come conveniently or inconveniently. For example, thoughts related to your personal life while you're at work or vice versa.

They can be linked to prejudices that can be very powerful. Prejudice is something we have learnt. We are not born prejudiced, and prejudice has a very low energy frequency that makes it not very favourable for yourself, others, or the planet to be judgemental. It drags down the whole energy web. Thoughts and feelings are also connected to love. They can colour our entire worldview.

It's important to recognise that thoughts are just thoughts. They create feelings, which create actions, which accumulate into behaviour, creating who we are and what we do in the world.

Sometimes, thoughts create beliefs if we think the same thought so often that we eventually consider it a truth. A negative belief could be: I'm not good enough. The boss doesn't listen. Colleagues are anti-social. Society doesn't help me. The belief can also be positive: I love me. The boss always listens. Colleagues see and meet me. Society is there to help me.

The process runs in circles. Thoughts turn into feelings, which reinforce the belief. The belief then turns into actions, which in almost all cases are actions that provide proof of the belief. No matter what we think, we create beliefs with a pattern that can either go down or up, be helpful or prevent us from living the life we want.

Thoughts, feelings, and beliefs are our minds. You could also say that thoughts, feelings, and beliefs are part of our consciousness, which means they are also part of our energy and are something that is really complex and come in many forms. Because our consciousness is an experience of what we think, which affects the emotions and actions that naturally follow.

Thoughts rush in and out of the brain. They are the language of the brain, whereas emotions are in the body. Here, we can feel joy or sadness. Emotions are the language of the body.

Consequently, beliefs and prejudices reside in both the brain and the body because they are fuelled by both thoughts and emotions. If we were only equipped with our brains, things would be dull and boring unless we were unbelievably good at being and thinking positively. The somewhat hidden driving force is unconditional love. Love is the language of the soul and a special and important partner.

In professional leadership, thoughts, feelings and beliefs help build culture and well-being. They arc fundamental elements when we build relationships and collaborate. And in many ways, this is what creates a shared endeavour – a company.

Good questions for management:

- Is it legitimate to talk about emotions in management and the organisation?
- What is the culture like? Is it emotionally cold, with a closed heart and soul, or emotionally warm, with an open heart and soul?

- Do management and leaders engage in open dialogue based on thoughts, feelings and beliefs?
- Is the culture embedded in the executive board?

In personal leadership, you also bring your physical, mental, and spiritual skills into play by embracing your true self and recognising that a thought is really just a thought.

For example, if it's a bad thought, it doesn't have to become anything more than a bad thought. That's it. If it's a bad feeling, what thought is behind it, and what could you put in its place?

Your feelings and thoughts are your responsibility. Period. They are never anyone else's responsibility, and no one can make you feel anything because your feelings stem from your thoughts.

Specifically, you can focus on.

- What beliefs am I struggling with?
- What thoughts and emotions am I struggling with?
- Where in my body are the emotions and beliefs that are speaking?
- If you encounter resistance in discussions, what are your underlying beliefs?
- Which beliefs trigger negatively and positively, and what could be the cause?
- Could you learn something if you were curious about your own thinking and that of others rather than looking at it as right and wrong

Exercise 10 at the back of the book can also be helpful.

You should be particularly aware of your feminine and masculine energies (see the section on dualism in Chapter 6) and learn to balance them in relation to your thoughts, feelings and beliefs. Recognising and understanding the feminine and masculine energy you use – especially when you're under pressure, because that's when the unpolished version of us comes out, and there's a lot of good stuff to work on. Taking on victim and martyr roles, for example, is unbalanced feminine energy and a great indicator of where you can look for answers to the challenges you are experiencing.

Relationships

Relationships are many things. It is the relationship with yourself. It is the relationship with other people. It can be work relationships, and it can be family. It can be something in the local neighbourhood. It can also be something in your country. It can be something global.

Your relationships also include more abstract relationships, such as your relationship with your self-esteem, with your self-confidence, and with nature and its resources. By relationships, we mean all the contexts and connections you are part of.

Relationships can be very different. You may encounter people who are introverted and some who are extroverted. There can be trust and love. You can be met, seen, heard and understood. You can also be rejected. You can be talked down to. You can feel left out. You can feel bullied. It can be about friends and colleagues, and it can be about your boss. It can be about children and siblings. It can be about parents. About partners. And co-workers.

Relationships are important because we are social beings, unlike animals, which don't have quite the same social needs as humans. Relationships create culture and are instrumental in creating work environments that are productive, healthy and meaningful.

Relationships create and drain energy. We are nourished or starved by relationships. If I have a good relationship with myself without guilt and shame, it creates a better energy frequency. The same is true in work relationships. Or a relationship for an entire population. The more love, humanity and compassion there is in the relationship, the better the (invisible but very noticeable) energy frequency, which raises the level of the entire energy web. Good relationships and good energy are contagious among "energy beings".

In terms of professional leadership, relationships are the glue of the organisation, and culture is probably the biggest and most important competitive factor, as it is difficult and takes a long time to replicate.

Good questions for leaders to ask themselves are:

- How are the relationships in the organisation?
- Does the employee satisfaction survey accurately reflect reality?
- Does everyone dare to talk openly about good and bad relationships?
- Does management have the courage to change something?
- How is the relationship with customers – from their point of view? The distance? The frequency? The quality?
- How is the relationship with suppliers and strategically important business partners?
- How could relationships (collaboration) become a true competitive parameter?

In personal leadership, relationship management is all about being authentic. It may be a rather tired word these days, but it's really about being (in touch with) yourself and being present. It's about balancing and recognising your self-worth and confidence and acting with an awareness of your integrity. To be your integrity. This appearance can be trained, both physically, mentally and spiritually.

Leaders can ask themselves:

- Am I showing up with authenticity and integrity?
- What are the biggest challenges I experience in relation to myself? (there are always some)
- What are the biggest challenges I experience in relation to others? (there are always some)
- Why do I think this is?
- Do I talk to anyone about it?

Relationships now and in the future are multidimensional. Multidimensionality entails the ability to connect the energetic, the physiological factors, intelligence, and healthy and harmonious ways of generating trustful creative power. It is exciting, complex, and challenging for all of us. To be a multidimensional person or company in balance with oneself, the surroundings, and work colleagues requires a special new stamina that can flow effortlessly and gently.

Relationships become the test of whether we succeed in our mission for humanity here on earth. To co-create in trust and harmony.

CHAPTER 4

Business fundamentals

Product

If there is no product, there is no business. In some businesses, the product may be linked to a passion, a calling, a cause. Other times, the product is created out of a spotted commercial opportunity that isn't necessarily linked to a personal passion.

A product can be physical, digital, or a service. Or a combination. It can be for citizens, it can be for customers. There can be basic editions, silver editions and gold editions. There's a design – a look – attached to it.

There is profitability and perhaps ongoing development or customisation for the specific customer. There's process and delivery. There are unique selling points: USPs. There's product journey, distribution, quality and longevity.

There is the technical and non-technical. There are customer needs. There may be social responsibility in production or delivery. There may be waste and disposal issues. There are ideas, research, development and testing. There are subcontractors and security of supply.

Responsible management is about sustainability. Fulfilling a need. Being competitive. Minimising waste. Maximising value. Creating a sense of meaningfulness among customers and employees. To play a real role and leave a positive footprint in the world.

A company can consider:

- Is the product future-proof, or are we too short-term in our development, value creation and marketing?
- Is it sustainable and in line with the company's purpose?
- Is the product important for future earnings?

- Does the organisation believe in the product?

For a product manager or anyone responsible for the product, it's important to use the full palette of new leadership and bring energy and heart into the process of creating and maintaining a product.

A product is not just something technical with materials and design/look but also something rooted in the company's soul and purpose. This is very much an area where new trends should be taken seriously – and much earlier in the strategy and development process than today.

Is the product being created in a way that recognises that users and customers are changing and have different needs than before? Let's look at some industry-specific examples.

- Travel industry: What we want on holiday is changing. We want nature, joy, tranquillity, and learning. And we want to arrive, eat, and interact sustainably. How does this affect the industry's products?
- The restaurant industry: Our dining experience is changing. We want community, nature, sustainability through local products, less alcohol, and more experiences. How do you create products and business models for that?
- Pharmaceutical industry: Our view of health is changing dramatically. We can no longer do the old model and don't want to stuff ourselves with medication unless it's absolutely necessary. We want to be truly healthy from within, curing ourselves as much as possible. We want prevention, not symptom management. So how does the industry's business model and products fit this paradigm shift, and is it aligned with the corporate and collective purpose

A product must also be saleable; you need money to run a business. Sales will also be affected by the new trends. As people and therefore customers change, disciplines like sales need to keep up. How we sell and buy will change, as the relationship will be built on trust, not fear or FOMO – fear of missing out. We will reflect more about what we really need and from whom we buy it.

Special attention should, therefore, be paid to push selling. In short, it no longer works with the game's new rules. Together with sales and marketing people, product people should look at the approach and language of sales:

- What words could be added to product and sales to emphasise awareness of the new trends and new customer needs?
- What energy resides in the sales methods and words used, and do they fit the purpose and values of both the organisation and the customer?
- How can decision-making processes include breaks to make decisions based on the most balanced energy and presence for both customer and salesperson?

Goal setting

In almost every organisation, goals are set. Most often because, we need to define a budget and align expectations with the board, each other and ourselves. Many recommend setting "smart" goals. Meaning they are specific, measurable, ambitious, realistic and time-bound.

Goals can be well managed or poorly managed. They can be about competition and fulfilment. They can be about money. They can be about communication. Goals are linked to the vision, mission and strategy, and the associated budget. There can be goals that are "must-win battles" and essential for survival, as well as goals that are softer and more nebulous.

In the latter part of the industrial age, everything has been a "burning platform" with "must-win battles" and "task force" teams in "war rooms". An organisation becomes deaf to the, unfortunately, often-used war rhetoric when it's in its 15th year. It's not nice to be at war all the time. War and fear are low-energy words, and the words we use impact our energy.

Instead of talking about the 'decade of crises', we could choose to get excited about the fact that there are plenty of opportunities to build a new world. Because the world is not broken. It's being made. And we choose whether we want to go up or down in energy, rhetoric, words and language, including when we work with goal setting.

We often have a lot of goals in a company. Do we dare to try having fewer goals, or perhaps no goals at all? And do we dare to eliminate the goals that have been on our nice posters for years but that we clearly have no passion for pursuing?

And could we start by deleting the crazy ones, like only talking to a customer for x minutes? Is there any chance they create good energy for customers and employees? Does it create a good customer experience? And is it sustainable if we look at it from a nervous system perspective?

I promise it's quite innovative when you look at a company's goals through the lens of energy. Where do goals energise us, and where do they wear out our energy, nervous system, and intuition? Where do they destroy our belief in the company's values and principles? Where do they contradict what we actually end up doing?

In management, it's important to focus and, of course, manifest the intention you have:

- What is the principle of the goals the company has?
- Do the goals support both the company's purpose and the culture employees want to be a part of?
- What language and words are used to communicate the goals?
- Does the organisation measure what is relevant, and is what is relevant measurable?
- Do the goals make sense to management and the organisation?
- How much time does the organisation spend on reporting, does it add value – and for whom?
- Do we have goals to motivate employees and managers to achieve their goals? And if so, why is this necessary?
- Are physical, mental and spiritual health measured?
- Are the goals ambitious and meaningful enough to engage the right people?
- Are the goals ambitious enough regarding the contribution they could potentially make to solving some of the world's, or local community's, problems?

Meaningful goal setting is a task for all management functions. Of course, finance, HR, and business controlling also have a special role to play. Most people take the task of goal setting seriously – especially now that ESG reporting is becoming part of everyday life in the EU.

It's a bit more challenging when it comes to personal goals:

- What is the balance between your personal soft goals (behavioural progress) and your personal hard goals (smart goals like sales, delivering a project by a certain time, number of units invoiced)?

- Are they goals that motivate you?
- Are they goals you have a say in?
- Do you measure your physical development (energy, sick days, medication use, weight, sleep, exercise)?
- Do you measure your mental development (less racing thoughts, less anger, less irritability, less prejudice, less conflict)?
- Do you measure your spiritual development (time for silence, clarity about what you want to do with your life, good habits)?
- Are your goals supported by your intuition and intention?

Data and technology (IT)

We all love IT when it works and we all hate IT when it doesn't. IT is becoming a nerve centre of our lives. At least the technical nerve.

Hardware, software, internet, gadgets, space, cables in ground and water, and satellites in space. It's vital, and it's difficult for us or easy for us. It helps create customer systems, financial systems and administration systems. It's a "drug" for us. It's a competitive force. It's also development, with the latest additions being artificial intelligence (AI), which we all need to learn to manage and utilise. We have virtual reality (VR), augmented reality (AR) and a metaverse on the way, which can be difficult to relate to.

Above all, technology provides a global interface and is the glue that connects us all, linking us to suppliers, customers and a host of people we know and don't know. IT increases globalisation and our outlook. It is also a world-class time waster.

However, we also have an interface to our consciousness that increases with the evolution of our IT use. Yes, that's a bold use of the word interface. Had it not been for technological development, it would have taken much longer to develop our consciousness. Because consciousness is having an experience – a movement of experiences. It's growing significantly and at an increasing rate; as we are more and more online, we can create more and new relationships quickly and easily. We can gain knowledge and sell our knowledge and products easier and faster. And we can experience distant realities, imaginary worlds, and test scenarios with just a few clicks.

So technology contributes to developing businesses and people, streamlining the value chain, giving us global reach, and scaling up the business.

When done correctly, it helps improve our processes and communication and the customer, employee, and citizen experience. It also helps automate routine tasks, reduce waiting time, and analyse information so we can make smarter decisions.

This is the good side of technological development and the natural task of the professional manager with responsibilities in areas such as IT and production.

A business leader can ask themselves:

- Is the digitalisation of the company taking place with a human focus?
- What role will artificial intelligence (AI) play?
- Does the company discuss ethical matters related to the development?
- Do we adequately relate to and keep up to date with user trends and new technologies – and do we ensure that our biases, preferences and habits don't dictate what we think the market wants?
- How do we ensure we understand the IT needs and preferences of newer generations?

Professional IT leaders need to work on the following:

- How do we ensure decision-makers have the right knowledge?
- How do we open management's eyes to the implications of, for example, AI? And the opportunities?
- How do we best uncover systemic biases and ethical issues?
- How should IT contribute to the triple bottom line? For example, do we have unnecessary, energy-intensive processes, hardware and systems?

- How can we increase security if employees work in multiple organisations or as project employees in the future?

On a personal level:

- How can I use IT to make Energetic Leadership more accessible?
- How do I deal with the ethical aspects of using artificial intelligence (AI) in my own life and at work?
- How can I take my own experience with Energetic Leadership and apply it to my work?

HR and the organisation

HR is often a funny thing that gets thrown around the organisation all the time. In many organisations, HR is sometimes in the thick of things and part of the management team at a high strategic level, and other times, HR is excluded from the management team and seen as a department that just takes care of payroll. A cost centre.

But times are such now that a potent HR function is vital to creating a future-relevant organisation that can attract and retain the right skills and create the new organisational structures employees want. HR has become more strategically important than ever before.

HR is about people, recognising and understanding people's needs, wants, and frustrations. It's about the employee journey, competencies and resources, talents and profiles. It's about communication and law and about development and employer branding.

But it's especially about the new energetic culture and creating the conditions for the "playground", the organism, the communi-teams

(teams that are self-led in creating a vibrant community), that talented employees actually want as their future workplace.

In professional leadership, HR helps set direction and define frameworks, roles, guidelines, and policies. HR helps put together the team and create the conditions for a culture that can unlock the organisation's potential in the short and long term.

So, what an HR leader and management in general can ask themselves is:

- How do we develop the organisation when we have four very different generations in the workplace?
- How do we create a meaningful framework for both those who are heading towards retirement in the foreseeable future and the younger generations who already do not emphasise the same values and are practising quiet quitting or resigning in droves?
- What must the workplace look like in 10 years time when it is almost entirely dominated by newer generations?
- How do we avoid falling behind on structural changes, such as the need for life breaks?
- How will knowledge be retained if the average tenure in a company drops significantly?
- How do we share and, at the same time, protect knowledge if employees have multiple jobs?
- How can we attract the best minds who also want to be self-employed on an equal footing with their job here? (the end of the concept of secondary employment, it's a desire on par with employment)

- What should the organisation's employee engagement strategy be? What makes an employee want to stay with the organisation for more than just three years?
- How can we legitimise and prioritise energy work so that health, well-being and creativity become the biggest competitive advantage?

If your role is somewhere in HR, it's your job to assess the extent to which management itself practises what you want from the organisation:

- Do you have the courage to be critically constructive?
- Do you understand the trends of the future and the consequences they have?
- Does management do what they say (walk the talk)?
- Is there a balance between the use of masculine and feminine energy in management and the organisation?
- What is management doing to develop themselves? Do they wait to be sent on a leadership course, or do they ask for feedback themselves and are proactive about personal development?
- Does management listen to and respond to the needs of the organisation?
- Do they recognise their own talents?
- Do they work from a talent mindset that is based on the genius zone that every person has?
- Is there a focus on measuring both the measurable and the noticeable when discussing KPIs? Is there a focus on integrating all three bottom lines in the business strategy?
- Are people a good representative of the area they work in?

- Are you and management a good representative of the culture you want to create?
- Is management a good representative of the set of climate goals?
- Is management a good representative of the physical, mental and spiritual health wanted in the organisation?

If you're a manager or specialist in an HR function, you also have a responsibility to lead the way, not just for your employees or colleagues, but for the entire organisation:

- What are you doing to learn more about yourself?
- What are you doing to be physically healthy?
- What are you doing to be mentally healthy?
- What do you do to be spiritually healthy and in touch with your soul?

In the chapter on constructive behaviour, you'll find plenty of tips on what you can do once you've identified your action points.

Health and finances

Finances are the foundation of any business. If there is no money in the bank, there is no business either.

It's good and important to have solid finances, with management keeping an eye on both short- and long-term income and expenses, as well as liquidity. Management must understand the numbers in depth and what it takes financially to create the development the company wants. Development requires capital. The financial foundation must be strong enough to withstand some of the external crises that will inevitably occur but also to include a so-called "fuck-up" buffer.

Reporting is no longer what reporting was. Therefore, measurement, target setting, and control are not what they used to be. According to EU legislation (not the UK), all large and listed companies are required to report on ESG, and later, also medium-sized and small companies. As previously mentioned, ESG is the new sustainable reporting with three bottom lines, which, in addition to financial accounting, also includes social and climate accounting. ESG reporting or not, these considerations are now an unequivocal demand from both consumers and employees.

It's no secret that a healthy economy creates jobs, development, and progress, and it's important to focus on both the short and long term. It's also important to have competent financial resources so that you don't tumble with your finances. Most people have that part under control.

However, finance lacks a focus on the human side of the agenda, so finance is not just about numbers. It also requires a human understanding of finance's new role. It helps to create change, not just as the passive passenger who first calls out when things are about to go wrong, but as the proactively involved who understands what the organisation can and wants – and how.

A management team can ask themselves:

- ESG reporting increases the focus on the finance function. How do we handle the fact that now both financial, social and climate issues regarding the company's potential must be commented on and discussed at board meetings?

- How do we ensure that we move from being a measurable business to a measurable and noticeable business where we can measure inner sustainability as well-being, care, and psychological and mental well-being?
- How do we measure the value of time, culture and communities?
- As the finance department's reporting and counselling increases, it puts pressure on finance management to understand what it means for the organisation to move from being mechanical to human.

A finance leader can consider the following questions.

- Do we know and understand the company and the employees we report on?
- Do we understand financially and in budgetary terms what being a productive, efficient and humane workplace means?
- How is the finance department itself a role model for the budget goals around humanity?

Values and principles

Where finance is the hard, concrete part of the foundation we can best relate to, values and principles are on the softer and "fluffy" end. Values and principles are like the mortar that holds the bricks together. Let me give a few very different examples.

Values: Trust, humour and flexibility

Principles: Involvement, job satisfaction and diversity

Or:

Values: Growth, agility and focus

Principles: Efficiency, adults over 40 only and performance

Values and principles are what create the culture. Values and principles may be formulated and communicated to the organisation but are not necessarily in alignment with how the company acts or how the values are perceived. Especially if what is communicated is not followed through and followed up on by management.

There are many examples of companies with fine values and principles on their websites, but where the reality is different, which can be reflected in customer and employee attrition, poor finances, and liquidation. For these companies, it has been difficult – almost impossible – to create alignment, engagement, and creativity within the organisation.

There are also plenty of examples of the opposite: coherence between what the organisation says and what it does. And then there's the fact that many smaller organisations don't have any formulated values and principles at all, apart from the ones the owner-manager practises in everyday life.

If the values and principles are robust and well-grounded, they create the desired flow and glue. If, on the other hand, they are destructive and lack support, inertia builds up in the company, which can be paralysing for the individual and the group. That can lead to uncertainty about the company's survival. A company without values and principles is like a ship without a guardrail. You can go overboard in any direction.

Every organisation should ask themselves:

- Is our culture reflected in our values and principles?
- What energy do the words that describe our values and principles have? What thoughts, feelings and sensations do employees have when they hear these words and phrases?
- How do we establish a framework for our culture, now and in the future, with energy awareness?

When it comes to personal leadership, values and principles are the business of every leader and employee in the organisation because everyone either lives or fails to live the intended values – consciously or unconsciously. Or they live their own values, which are in better harmony with their inner self and/or their goals or life purpose.

As a person and leader, you can ask yourself:

- What are my values and principles?
- Do I stand by them when they are in a headwind?
- Do I stand by them when I'm under pressure?
- Do the company's values and principles match my own?
- Am I a good fit to be in this company?
- Does the company match my inner desires?
- If I'm not sure, why am I here?

Once you've taken stock, you can develop your competencies:

- What do I do if my values are challenged?
- If they are challenged, do I act in a balanced and harmonious way, or do I act unbalanced in an inappropriate way, e.g. with anger, closed-mindedness, or bullying?

Constructive behaviours

THE DUALITY BETWEEN FEMININE AND MASCULINE ENERGY FOSTERS VALUABLE BUSINESSES

Dualism (feminine and masculine energy)

When we are imbalanced in the use of our feminine and masculine energy, it can manifest in different ways:

- If we are predominantly masculine in our energy and behaviour, such as dominant, aggressive and selfish, we become unbalanced and can be perceived as a dictator or workaholic.
- If, on the other hand, we are predominantly feminine in our energy and behaviour, such as vulnerable, sensitive and giving, we are out of balance and can be perceived as a victim or a manipulative dreamer.

In a positive light, the energies are expressed like this:

- A person who is pure in their masculine energy will be perceived as a hero and protector with their strong, focused, and overbearing traits.
- A person who is pure in their feminine energy will be experienced as a creator and healer with their supportive, sensual and loyal traits.

For centuries, we have disconnected the feminine energy and exaggerated the masculine energy. Now, they need to integrate into a beautiful and healthy symbiosis. Both energies are always present. Being unbalanced means that we are too much in one energy. Being balanced means that we have natural fluctuations on both sides, but we manage to find our way back to the balance point. Read more about how to do this in the reset exercise at the back of the book.

Fluctuations happen, and that's okay. Life hits us all the time with things that break, challenging relationships, deaths, and other external crises. And we consciously choose to give it a go when a project or a book needs to be finished. What we need to train is awareness of the balance of energy, the ability to identify where we are, and the knowledge of what it takes to get back to zero – to the balance point.

Or, to put it another way, we need to be good at finding our way back to calmness in the nervous system and, thus, pleasant behaviour and fruitful, stress-free relationships with ourselves and others. Our behaviour is linked to our cells and DNA and, therefore, to how we feel physically, mentally, and spiritually.

Understanding what this dualism entails and why it's crucial is a prerequisite for learning how we act when we're in a state of flux, as well as for being able to understand the behaviour of others in our lives and the workplace.

Positive harmonious dualism is associated with good energy and flow, whereas unbalanced dualism creates dark energy, blockages, and distorted people.

People observe and learn from each other, and women have made a special effort to resemble men as they are in their leadership roles – but unfortunately, in many cases, they are unbalanced men. In other words, both genders are often imbalanced, with too little feminine energy.

Therefore, we must all seek to understand ourselves and our personal starting point and to develop and train based on that.

As leaders, with the influence and power that comes with the role, we also have a responsibility not to create a society and companies that primarily have leadership with masculine energy. The reason why it is important to create a balanced society is that a one-sided focus on one part, our productive part, makes us sick – because we are not machines. We are currently seeing all the signs of illness in the labour market in the form of dissatisfaction, distrust, lack of healthy growth and misuse of resources and time.

We need to work on how our working relationships, our teams and our cultures are conscious of balancing the two sides and recognise the problem of a sick labour market. A good and meaningful culture has both a "masculine" side (what we "do" together, such as team meetings and team building) and a feminine side (how do we do it, do we listen to employees, do we reflect on whether what we've been doing for 5 years still works, and do we dare to talk about it).

When we have a labour market with strong masculine traits, we must have the courage to discuss how we bring humanity (feminine) to the entire structure and culture. This duality is vital. Therefore, as leaders, we must dare to talk about it and take the initiative to talk about it. It can feel awkward at first because no one expects it to be on the agenda, but that's exactly why it's important. Relating it to purpose, values, principles, goals, and organisation is a good place to start.

As soon as we talk about the lack of focus on the feminine, the debate often gets heated. Don't. Because it's not anyone's fault. It's a condition. It's circumstances that have brought the world to this point, and now it's time to move on from here. Pointing fingers is not going to help anyone, but we have to recognise that we have been brought up in cultures that have been very masculine for generations, which means that there are things we have to unlearn and things we have to relearn – all of us.

As leaders, you should ask yourself:

- What is balanced feminine leadership?
- What is balanced masculine leadership?
- What does balanced leadership look like for us as a company, leader and team?
- How will we work with it?
- Do we understand the M/F energies well enough, and how can we work with them?

In your personal leadership, you can start with the following exercises:

- ☐ Write down the feminine traits that are primary for you, and write down the masculine traits that are primary for you.
- ☐ Which feminine traits play out when you are tired and stressed? And which masculine traits emerge when you are tired and stressed?
- ☐ What do you do to find balance when you're tired and stressed?

The ego as a dancing partner

In the quest to understand ourselves and our behaviour, we now turn to the ego, whom we want to teach a few new dance steps that will enable ego and soul to dance a close and passionate Argentine tango together, forgetting time and place. If we succeed, we "tame" the ego and use it in a good way, and we create a nurturing space where the soul is more comfortable. This helps to create an incredibly constructive platform for better behaviour, affecting ourselves and others.

We've already briefly touched on the ego in the story of Old Me and

New Me. Our ego can be a good ego or a bad ego. Or you could say that it can be in a good or bad mood, depending on which of its instincts are triggered.

We can learn to understand our ego, and we can learn to manage our ego. The ego is part of being human. It is an acting part of us.

It is our best friend because it wants to look after us, and it is also our worst friend because it wants to keep us in old (familiar, safe) patterns. The ego does this with the thoughts, words and phrases we hear inside. The ego can take a thought and go crazy with it if we can't stop that behaviour ourselves.

When we are unbalanced, with either too much masculine or feminine in our behaviour, the ego keeps us stuck in that role and behaviour. Like a little bandit, the ego says, "You can't stop being dominant and controlling because then you're weak" (masculine energy), or "You can't stop being supportive and sacrificing because then you're selfish" (feminine energy).

In other words, the ego rides the merry-go-round with us when we are unbalanced and boundary-less. In that situation, we can't hear the soul, and, therefore, we can't see through the windscreen. We become stowaways, reacting on a distorted autopilot.

When we talk about the ego, it's natural to also talk about the soul, as the two need to be friends – to be able to dance the tango. In the old leadership, they are often seen as opposites, but in the new energetic leadership, we understand the importance of cooperation between them.

As just mentioned, our feminine and masculine energy must be able to work together, and there must be room for both. When that's not in balance, we face challenges with our ego and soul. Because when we suppress the feminine and intuitive, we don't have access to the soul, and the bad ego takes over. If, on the other hand, we understand how to balance M/F, we gain unhindered access to the soul and can control the ego so that it is primarily used as a progressive and constructive driver.

Coach and clairvoyant medium Rikke Hertz has this fine alignment of ego and soul in her book.[62]

Where do you find yourself?

Ego – Soul

We want to be right	-	Is grateful
Compares	-	Is loving and affectionate
Wants power	-	Is inclusive and open
Wants to be in control	-	Is positive and curious
Wants prestige	-	Is in balance
Focuses on winning	-	Thinking win-win-win-win
Has an opinion on everything	-	Is authentic
Easily feels resistance and becomes irritable	-	Is calm
Is influenced by the opinions of others	-	Resting in oneself
Wants competition	-	Is accepting
Fear of failure	-	Is forgiving
Becomes envious and jealous	-	Gives freedom
Boasting	-	Trusts others
Holds grudges	-	Believes in something
Is aggressive	-	Is patient
Is passive-aggressive	-	Is happy for others
Displays anger	-	Feels hope

A management team can ask themselves:

- What does it take to create a harmonious leadership team?
- Do we have the courage to give each other constructive feedback?
- What is the first next step?

In personal leadership, most people can get to know themselves much better:

- Can you feel when your "bad" ego is leading you?
- Can you feel when your soul is leading you?

When doing the exercises in the back of the book, you might want to keep a notebook so you can write down and draw whatever comes to mind as you develop. You'll enjoy looking back on your quantum leaps!

- ☐ Use the exercises in the back of the book to calm down and listen quietly.
- ☐ Use exercise 9 to practise and understand how your body says yes and no from the ego and soul, respectively.
- ☐ Write down which actions and statements you are upset about, e.g. a statement you sent without sufficient thought. What triggered you? Forgive yourself for it. And acknowledge it to the person or people you took it out on.

Acknowledge your inner child

Up until the age of about three, a lot is created in us as human beings. Of course, we can't remember everything, yet our experiences and memories affect our body, which affects our mind, which in turn affects our soul.

So when we talk about the inner child, we all carry something in our luggage, and we all need to continue to look after our inner child and be aware of it.

The inner child is and has unconditional joy. We know nothing but joy until we start letting ourselves be influenced by others. And it is this joy that we must try to preserve and return to remember because it is unique.

Loving ourselves and our inner child is about finding our way back to the feeling and sensation in our body from which the joy originated. If you find a picture of yourself from when you were very young, hopefully, you can see the joy, the twinkle in your eye and the energy that exists in such a small, innocent child.

You may have experienced abandonment consciously, and you may also have been abandoned unconsciously. It happens to all of us to a greater or lesser extent, and abandonment is not necessarily only the extreme kind. It's also quite common to have been told wrongly no. We may need to find our way back to the state in which we experienced the betrayal, understand the feeling the betrayal created, and forgive ourselves or others.

But we can also fail the inner child ourselves. Sometimes, it's about behavioural patterns where we act in a way where the inner child is basically shouting, "No, don't do that, or say that, or feel that way". Our inner child is full of emotions and bodily discomfort that continue to surface as we grow into adolescents and adults. There is, therefore, a lot of help – self-help – to be gained when we take the time to understand these dynamics and understand what the emotions and discomfort are telling us.

The prerequisite for being able to set boundaries is to recognise your inner child and be aware of situations in which you are triggered by others, such as becoming upset, agitated, irritated, frustrated, angry, or self-destructive. These reactions tell you that your boundaries have been violated.

When you're in that situation, the best thing to do is to listen, say "hmm... interesting!" in your mind, and either withdraw or engage in a dialogue if you can do so constructively and clearly state where your boundaries are (e.g. I don't want you to talk to me like that again).

Then, the exercise is to find out what it is in you that makes you triggered. So it's not about pointing the finger at the person who triggered you, but more about why you had that reaction and how you can avoid it in the future. It teaches us where our boundaries are, and it can point us in the direction of our values and integrity.

The ball is in your court to take action on this and work on making sure your boundaries are strong and without gaps. The old way was that we felt violated; it was the other person's fault. We didn't have to change anything ourselves, it was the other person who had to fix themselves. The new currency is personal development, and we all need to develop. And since the feeling comes from your thoughts and the memory resides in your body, only you can do the job.

Regardless of where we belong in an organisation, our upbringing affects our adult life and, therefore, our working life. This can be expressed in thoughts, actions, and emotions, basically our behaviour.

In your leadership role, ask yourself:

- What fascinates you about working with people?
- How do you work with personal insights?

- Can you lead others if you don't like yourself, if you don't know yourself, or don't know how we humans work?

And for your personal leadership, you can spend time sensing how you feel in your body, with your thoughts and emotions:

☐ Make a daily note of how your energy feels; is it contracting or expanding? What gives and what takes energy?

☐ Also, note how good you are at listening to your body's reactions. Are there situations where you need to improve your listening skills?

☐ Notice in which situations you withdraw, remain silent, get angry, scold or snap. What could be the reason?

☐ Hug your inner child when you get upset. Tell it it's not alone, and you'll do everything you can to stop letting it down.

The body actually tells us with clear signs if there is something we don't like to do or say or if we are spoken to in a certain way. It doesn't have to be another person doing it. It could be yourself. Or it could be the things you don't do that you want to do that feel like a letdown.

Your conscious awareness (and, therefore, your connection to your soul) becomes much clearer when you are able to listen to your inner child.

Silence

I have invented a new concept because I didn't think there was one that covered what I needed. Namely, being actively present in silence. I call it silent listening.

It's not necessarily about mindfulness or meditation. It's about being quiet and listening inward. This means that you don't say anything.

You can be quiet by sitting/lying still with open or closed eyes. You can also be quiet by walking, just being silent, and not saying anything. It's simply a state where you consciously choose to be quiet and listen inward. This means that you consciously 'tune' your intention to be quiet and feel/listen/see what you experience in your body and your mind. Because only when we don't speak do we not use our capacity to find sentences that sound reasonable in our head or when we say them out loud. Only when you are quiet can you hear the inner true you and the voice of your soul.

You listen with all your senses to your breathing and observe the signs, words, images, and sounds that may occur. They can come from the outside world that you see. They can also come from within. Silent listening is noise-free. We often think there is a lot of noise in our lives, but here, you accept noise or being in noise without it affecting you.

Silent listening should be done daily. Everyone can do it, and it's easy, enjoyable and completely free. It's about caring for ourselves. You get a better sense of yourself, whether you're in pleasure or pain. And you get better at just feeling, listening and seeing, and letting your thoughts fly by. And in this way, you allow your soul to knock on the door and be heard. Allow it to come home.

For many people, being silent is almost anxiety-provoking, frightening, uncomfortable and bordering on socially unacceptable and rude. When we're with others, and no one is talking, it can feel imperative to break the silence.

Silent listening is the first step on the inner journey and can naturally lead you to more, such as meditation or being consciously present in your soul energy. You can use silent listening as your charging station.

In leadership, silent listening helps increase awareness and intuition and find home within yourself. It helps create better leadership and communities – and, therefore, better results – by understanding the body's signals. This is not the same as reflecting, which is an analytical process in the brain that usually aims to arrive at a result. Silent listening, on the other hand, doesn't create something new but brings out what we know deep down, provided the door is open to the soul.

In professional leadership, you can ask the following questions:

- Is silence accepted in the organisation?
- Is silence something that is talked about as both physical silence and inner silence?
- Are there quiet spaces in the organisation where you can sit peacefully and be still?
- Is it socially acceptable (even among managers) to step aside to quietly listen and connect with themself and their soul?
- Are silent listening exercises part of the staff policy and something actively encouraged?
- Are you measuring whether employees practise silent listening as much as sickness absence days?
- Has management said no to suggestions to increase silence within the last five years?
- Is silence prioritised in meetings before making a decision so that everyone can listen to whether it is the head that makes a decision or whether it is actually connected to the soul?
- Does management have the courage to create both quiet rooms and sound rooms as part of the company's facilities so that the physical conditions support the focus on an energy-based culture?

Quiet rooms are used to gather and recover energy by being quiet, either alone or with others.

Sound rooms are used to practise and develop your energy by sounding out the feelings and sensations you experience in your body. Guided meditations and sound healing can also be played.

Both quiet rooms and sound rooms are examples of the fitness spaces of the future.

In personal leadership, silent listening helps you to be more calm and conscious. And you can become better at responding to your body's signals and needs. In this way, it increases your ability to be in balance physically, mentally and spiritually.

You can become better at relying not only on brain-based understanding and the core disciplines of your profession but also on being connected to your body and intuition so that it's not just the rational part that counts.

In your personal leadership, I recommend:

- ☐ Hug your inner child, give it care and good energy.
- ☐ Practise silent listening daily in your favourite place (inside or outside).
- ☐ Note daily what changes you experience over time when you practise silent listening, e.g. by keeping a journal.

There are thorough instructions for silent listening in the back of the book.

To accommodate

In order to understand what it means to accommodate, it's important to first understand fear. Fear is a natural and biological part of every human being. We need to be able to take off and run fast when a tiger is chasing us. This rarely happens, though, so the fear we carry with us is mostly cultural.

For me, I'm afraid of not being good enough (we almost all are, by the way), afraid of going fast on cross-country skis when there are no tracks, afraid of being on the back of a motorbike and falling and hurting my neck, which I've struggled with a lot. For all humans, there will be something we're afraid of, consciously and unconsciously, and that's perfectly natural and okay.

What's not good is when that fear of something also becomes emotional because, in that case, those emotions start controlling us. In the worst-case scenario, it can become a self-fulfilling prophecy, as it affects our behaviour and can limit our room for manoeuvre and our potential. We are simply inhibiting ourselves.

Before we focus on accommodating, it's important to also understand projection. As a psychological concept, projection is the mechanism by which we unconsciously attribute to others some of the qualities we ourselves have and don't appreciate.

In in-depth psychology, the general rule of thumb is that 90% of the (bad) qualities you attribute to others actually belong to your own unconscious psyche.[63]

It's very beneficial to be aware that we all project to a greater or lesser extent. We all need to look at what is hidden under the iceberg – in our unconscious self.

Therefore, we have great benefits in learning to embrace our whole being. This is actually at the heart of the new energetic leadership.

Think of yourself (and everyone else) as a house. The house has some characteristics in the old leadership regime and others in the new energetic leadership. To clarify the difference, we can call the old leadership *Cabinet of Horrors* and the new one *Stronghold of the Soul.*

Characteristics

Cabinet of Horrors (ego rules – no contact with the soul)

- Little or no consciousness
- Hides all inner junk in the basement
- Constant fog
- Complex
- Wet and mouldy
- No development zone
- Hard to meet the inner child
- Debating ourselves
- Pressurised nervous system that speaks loudly
- The ego rules

Stronghold of the Soul (contact with the soul – ego & soul slow dancing)

- Conscious choice to want to be here
- All junk from the basement is up in the house, in the light
- Clarity
- Light and simple – almost magical

- Lush and beautiful
- Open for development
- Easy to meet the inner child
- No debate with ourselves
- Calm nervous system that is quiet
- The soul rules

The **basement** is home to everything we don't want to acknowledge or that we have healed and turned into something positive.

Cabinet of Horrors (ego rules – no contact with the soul)

- Personal, family, and collective trauma
- Shadow sides
- Prejudice and self-criticism
- Blocked energy
- Selfishness
- Intentions and actions in bad karma

Stronghold of the Soul (contact to the soul – ego & soul dance closely)

- Reconstructed basement, now with a home spa and orangery, which makes everything grow lushly and beautifully – because here we bring our true self along through trust, respect, and humanity – we are capable of accommodating ourselves and others.
- Conscious healing of trauma
- Shadow sides are out in the light
- Accommodate yourself and others
- Energy in flow
- Intentions and actions are from the soul

The **foundation** is expected mental (brain) values and principles.

Cabinet of Horrors (ego rules – no contact with the soul)

- Pseudo values
- Principles we "punch" through
- No or little involvement
- Brain and ego are in
- Intuition and honest intention is a rare guest
- Little reason to exist

Stronghold of the Soul (contact with the soul – ego & soul dance closely)

- True values
- Principles we actually practise
- Involvement and self-management
- Brain and soul symbiosis
- Intuition and intention symbiosis
- Strong raison d'être

The **rooms** are everything we do, try and believe we should in our lives.

Cabinet of Horrors (ego rules – no contact with the soul)

- We push through tasks in a mental, hard and unpeaceful way, with stomach aches and stress
- Growth, power and money
- Knowledge
- Hasty and inefficient
- Lots of conflicts, resolved in fear
- The human head is in charge
- More and more

Stronghold of the Soul (contact to the soul – ego & soul dance closely)

- We flow easily and enjoyably between each other, and tasks are solved with enthusiasm and smiles on our faces
- Regenerative growth and co-creation
- Wisdom
- Smart and efficient
- Few conflicts, resolved in trust
- Nature guides
- Better and better

To accommodate oneself and others is to accommodate the whole house and all the floors. To embrace your experiences, feelings, thoughts, prejudices, beliefs, and assumptions. To forgive yourself. To forgive others. To forgive experiences. But also to know that others must accommodate themselves.

You do this by accepting yourself and others. As mentioned, the starting point is that we are each responsible for ourselves and cannot point fingers and say or think that it's everyone else's fault. Not regarding situations, feelings or thoughts.

We are the ones who are responsible, and we are the ones who have to accommodate ourselves and our thoughts and feelings. Someone may have behaved in a way they shouldn't have, but that's really their own business, and it's up to us to decide what it means and whether it matters at all. To accommodate is to refrain from identifying with the feeling you experience when you're treated unfairly, no matter how unfair it is.

When you learn to tolerate the negative feelings you get from an unfair experience, you help yourself have better energy (a better frequency) by not exposing your system to more than you can handle.

When you're not good at accommodating, all the unfair experiences you've had take up capacity in your system (like on a computer), e.g., old traumas, stress from the workplace, noise, radiation, accusations from other people (private and professional), circumstances such as corona, war or unemployment. Or your own negative self-talk.

This can either result in a breakdown, like a computer shutting down, or in inappropriate behaviour. The inappropriate behaviour often comes from not being self-aware enough because your ego keeps telling you that you should be doing better. You get angry or upset, which is really a defence against the emotions you can't contain.

When we're more aware of how to accommodate, it creates better understanding, better relationships, and better well-being, and it energises ourselves and others.

An inclusive relationship with yourself and others is free of prejudices and assumptions. This way, you gain better energy, resulting in better vibrations and frequency, which helps to build rather than destroy. Remember that positive energy attracts more positive energy, and negative energy attracts more negative energy.

In professional leadership, you can ask:

- What does it take to accommodate the new generations and their differences?
- What does it take to accommodate the rebels?
- What does it take to create a bridge of trust, from the Cabinet of Horrors to the Stronghold of the Soul, between management and employees?

And in more personal leadership, it's good to gain insight by observing and noting how you react.

- Can you accommodate yourself and your professional leadership?
- Can you accommodate the company's leadership?
- Are you aware that you are the only one responsible for you and your emotions?
- Do you tend to blame others or the system?
- How do you deal with uncomfortable situations?

Observing and taking notes is one thing, but practice makes perfect.

☐ Note physical and mental senses in yourself and others and learn from them. You need to train yourself so that subsequent thoughts and emotions don't disturb you.
☐ Praise yourself and hug your inner child.

Communities

Humans are social herd animals; ever since we have been on this earth, we have needed communities. We have needed each other. We thrive on being together. It's not just about warming each other up in a cold hut. It's about so much more than warmth and reproduction. It's about being part of the herd because we don't like being outside the herd; it makes us lonely, and we can lose the spark of life. At our deepest roots, we have an ancient belief that surviving alone is almost impossible.

Communities can be experienced in many ways. They can be local, they can be national, they can be global. They can be the workplace, a professional network or family. They can be through interests and hobbies, and they can be through things we care about, like sustainability, peace and war (or whatever is generally on the agenda that interests us), or football. Communities are the foundation of making social people thrive.

It may seem strange that this needs to be said, but in professional leadership, people are still social beings. They are not machines. Over the last 100 years, we've seen HR evolve in this way, with people in organisations going from being a 'commodity' to a 'resource' to a 'family' and now to being human beings in a regenerative, self-regulating ecosystem. We are social beings energised by togetherness and presence.

Community helps to create good energy, which means it affects our health. And it affects our innovation and creativity, producing happiness and good health. Joy is the biggest driver of human well-being, both in the small daily magic moments and the big magic moments.

Communities are the core of energy and relationships. They are also the redeeming factor and our basic premise that liberates us to dare to be who we are when we experience being seen, met, heard and understood in the herd and by the management and supported in what we live and work for.

Communities must be approached voluntarily and built on respect, inclusion, and trust. A community that is a dictatorship or otherwise forced is not a community, neither in the democratic understanding nor in the human sense.

Late modern society will, to a much greater extent, be built on communities and partnerships. The pace of development is so fast that in order to keep up, we need to share knowledge through collaboration and partnerships.

In the future, no one will succeed alone, but only together, and there are several reasons for this:

1. More people bring more ideas, competencies and energy into play, for example, in research and development.
2. Development is so fast that no one can know everything, and we need each other's competencies.
3. Strengths and areas for development (vulnerabilities) are natural premises. The dualism of including both sides in everything that is created and delivered is natural.
4. The 17 SDGs and the entire sustainability agenda, both the external and the internal, are the foundation for a global and local community.
5. Changing organisational forms are creating new ways of organising work and the entire sourcing process, creating new effective partnership models built on much higher levels of trust.
6. The world's significant global geopolitical and economic challenges can be alleviated through a foundational undercurrent of partnerships among the public, private sector, and citizens.

Professional leadership can ask:

- Is the organisation a community?
- What characterises the company's community?
- Are employees involved in discussions about the company's future community?
- Does management contribute to the community?

In personal leadership, it's important to listen to your physical body, mental mind, and spiritual soul. So listen to your intuition and the energy that tells you where you feel it's good to be and why.

- ☐ Note which communities you enjoy and why.
- ☐ Decide if there are any that need to end.
- ☐ Are you contributing to the community – the immediate and the collective?

CHAPTER 6

Evolving operations

Insight

Insight is linked to the business and consists of all the knowledge that a company can gain internally (by listening at the coffee machine or through analysis or measurements) or externally (future foresight, what the market looks like, and what your customers are saying). In other words, it includes all insights into the market situation, the company's industry, the company itself, and especially how the company is doing internally.

Insight is also about being equipped with knowledge about the development and transformation you want. It's about policy, law, energy, intuition, involvement, and research. It's about qualitative and quantitative analyses, focus groups, curiosity, feedback, knowledge, wisdom, development, creation, innovation and creativity, being open and listening, asking and understanding.

In organisations, it's easy for insight to be under-prioritised and for people not to take the time to gather relevant knowledge. This is a problem in itself, but more importantly, the old leadership was primarily built on rational, professional "head" knowledge. The new leadership connects intuitive wisdom with rational knowledge, thereby strengthening insights, decisions and outcomes.

Today, we can't know everything professionally. Intuitive knowledge can strengthen leadership development and communication. Professional and intuitive knowledge is the winning cocktail for understanding the future and how managers should be able to lead the organisation along new paths.

Here are some questions leaders can ask themselves:

- What does it take for management to gain the insights they need?
- What internal and external insights does management have?
- Does management dare to gather insights from unconventional sources and people?
- Does management trust intuitive knowledge?
- Does the organisation have people dedicated to foresight activity?

It's also important to consider your own approaches:

- Where are my blind spots?
- Which biases do I have?
- What do I do to minimise bias and blind spots?
- Do I find it easy to develop and expand my perspective and gain new insights? If not, what's holding me back?
- What kind of insights am I gaining?
- What knowledge about myself do I hesitate to gain or recognise, and why?

Questions are great, but intuitive listening really trumps.

- ☐ Do the silent listening exercise for 20 minutes and ask your inner self what you need.

The customer journey and delivery

The customer journey and customer delivery tie the entire company together across departments because the entire company and organisation is involved in developing, implementing, and delivering products and services to customers.

This is true whether it's a customer journey, a citizen journey, or an employee journey. Experience, loyalty drivers and touchpoints must be defined and designed to increase frequency and energy.

What characterises a customer journey (or should we call it a customer web as it is not linear) with a customer delivery is that it reflects the company's strategic decision to be customer-centric, including the thoroughness with which you develop, implement, and report on the work that weaves the organisation together.

If we consider the customer journey as the company's energy web, it also illustrates how important it is that the grid is intact so that energy can flow effortlessly through it.

The customer journey (and the energy grid it represents) is the invisible image of the community and collaboration that exists within an organisation. If relationships are poor (internally and externally), energy is blocked, and work is done sluggishly, or not at all.

The core of the customer journey is the delivery, defined as the benefits of the product, service, price, distribution, brand & marketing, and sustainability. An overall value proposition to the customer that is both meaningful and valuable to the need and draws on an underlying concrete description of what the customer can expect to be delivered.

The customer experience is challenged. CX expert Ian Wisler-Poulsen explains[64]:

> "Customer experience has been de-prioritised in certain areas. Change is fast-paced, professionalism and technological capabilities are exploding, and so services are often complex. Customers don't necessarily know much about what they are buying today, so the experience will become more important to the customer because that is what they can relate to."

The customer experience is the lifeblood of organisational well-being and should be a top priority, strategically, tactically and operationally. Customer value should be described *rationally*, i.e. concretely in terms of units, time, numbers, etc. But also *irrationally*, i.e. experience and sensation in the body in the form of thoughts, emotions, energy and other bodily sensations that must be created at every single contact point on the customer journey.

The underlying description covers processes and guidelines, IT systems, roles, and competencies, as well as follow-up and reporting. Prerequisites for a well-oiled delivery system.

Professional leadership has the potential to take growth and loyalty drivers to a whole new level with focus, stamina and a long-term perspective.

The strategic analysis should include:

- What will it take for the business to be strategically driven, with the customer journey and delivery as a focal point?
- What drives the delivery and energy of the touchpoint?
- What creates energy and loyalty for the customer?
- What energises and engages the employee?
- Are there differences in what drives value perception and loyalty in different customer segments?

Everyone in the organisation should know the journey, the delivery, their role in the process and what it takes to make it all work.

So a leader can ask themselves:

- Are the efforts to be 100% customer-centric anchored in top management?
- Does management understand the company's product and overall delivery?
- Is customer work seen as a hygiene factor (part of the basics) or a special project or programme?
- Who owns customer work in management and on the board?
- Do we measure both rational and irrational customer value?

Who is responsible for delivering and developing the customer journey can be very different. For example, it could be in a marketing department, a separate business unit, a product department, an IT and development department, a go-to-market department, or spread across multiple departments.

Whether you have full or partial responsibility, try the following:

- Print out the entire journey for the customer – all documents and communications from advertising to the follow-up routine after the customer's onboarding and departure. Lay it all out in a long strip so you physically see the entire delivery. Does it match the intent? Is everything meaningful and energising from an objective customer and company perspective?
- Is the journey easy and clear for the customer and yourself, and is there a good energy flow for both parties?
- Are there low-hanging fruit that can be harvested?
- Are there IT systems that are so complex that you've almost given up on solving important challenges, such as correcting errors on invoices or in direct emails to customers?
- Is AI being used in a valuable and ethical way?
- Does everyone in the organisation understand that there is a concrete physical deliverable and a relational and intuitive deliverable? Is this described in processes and guidelines – and are employees trained in both?

If you're a manager, you can also:

- ☐ Test how your energy impacts the customer experience.
- ☐ Observe the energy of customer service staff.
- ☐ Assess what it takes to take the customer journey and delivery to the next level.

Marketing

Marketing is, of course, about taking your product to market through advertising, PR and campaigns to create visibility for the product and company and nudge customers to buy in every possible way. But it's also about understanding customer needs and having a deep understanding of the mindset and emotions that drive a customer to buy a company's products.

Marketing is changing as everything else is changing, and digitalisation, in particular, is playing a huge role, with lots of new ways to market and new players and media in the market. Most recently, we have had to consider the use of artificial intelligence (also customers' use of, e.g., ChatGPT and Bard), the metaverse, security issues around TikTok, and an increasing number of hacker attacks that make us vulnerable in our online behaviour.

The novel phenomenon in marketing will be the "invisible" driver – the energy. Because what happens in marketing when both customers and marketing employees no longer think that fear-based and push marketing is fun? They know that customers don't want it; many are turning off advertisements and are happy to pay to avoid the influence. At the same time, there is a growing awareness that we don't actually need many of these products. And marketing employees feel the same way as consumers.

There is a real risk that the work they used to be proud of no longer makes sense. And there's also a risk that yesterday's leaders are taking too long to realise that new, more communicative and helpful marketing is needed – and often less measurable. It has become harder to get attention, and right now, it's also harder to measure it because the conversation about the company primarily takes place between customers and in fragmented micro-conversations. You could say that we're now in an Attention Economy.

Marketing will be based more on the positive energy of trust in the future. Not because it sounds good in our planning, but because when we get into better and better balance, we don't listen to our fear anymore. Now, we can and dare to make good, meaningful decisions. We are increasingly experiencing resistance to aggressive sales and marketing tactics.

Marketing becomes about language and emotional and rational customer types. It's about brand and identity and a reimagined brand platform. It's about the essence and storytelling of your why and bringing purpose into play throughout the organisation. It's about integrity and ethics.

Marketing is moving from being aggressive and inhuman to being sensitive and human. And the vast majority of companies have to go through everything because almost no one today has energy as a starting point. There is no way around it if the company wants to remain relevant in the market, and we are to retain the most talented employees who have future-sense and understand how to navigate the new world.

Marketers must bring themselves and their energy into play in a whole new way and dive deep into understanding what energetic intelligence is: a new language and a new communication. If you don't understand it yourself – not with your head, but with your body, mind and soul – it's difficult to understand the change that is currently in full swing in the market, how it should be reflected in your communication, which should be much more emotional communication. In this context, there is also a new dimension to segmentation, which is based on emotional customer types.[65] [66] [67]

Some readers may think that it is necessary to sell and convince customers. It is important to say that it is not a question of not selling, but that sales must be redefined to be about helping customers make a choice: a clear objective recommendation, which is thus a clarification of whether the two parties are a good fit (customer-organisation and customer-product). Instead of pushing a sale, the runway is laid out for an energetic match sale or a sale between two people with the same heart and soul on the same frequency. This doesn't mean you don't want to sell and don't want to make money. But the way you do it will change in the future.

Marketing managers can ask themselves:

- What role has marketing played in leadership, strategy and culture in the past, and what is the desired role in the future?
- Is marketing happening on autopilot? Or is it truly innovative, focusing on the trends currently changing the market's needs, wants and ways of acting (and interacting)?
- Should our communication be adjusted to better recognise customers' energy awareness and rebelliousness?

On a personal level, the questions could be:

- How does your development affect your role in marketing?
- Have you articulated your life purpose?

Execution

Execution here has two meanings: the execution of programmes, projects, and initiatives linked to a strategy and the actual process and delivery of the deliverable to the customer.

The strategic part, which consists of programmes, projects, and initiatives, is fundamental. It helps ensure that the strategy comes to life and is a stepping stone to the new level you have decided on.

At the same time, development is useless if you can't deliver the basics effectively and efficiently. And here, we can go beyond the product itself because the brand is part of the customer delivery. If you don't talk about who you are as a company, and if the basic processes for ordering, payment, delivery and customer service don't work, it affects the customer experience. Effective execution is essential, as this is where the company builds the relationship with the customer and the customer's intention to return.

Execution is easily perceived as content and schedules. And in a way, it is. You can and should take a brain approach to execution, but you also need to take a heart-and-soul approach to it. Old-fashioned execution with professional knowledge, best practices, standard procedures and fixed schedules is no longer sufficient – if it ever was – because, in many cases, it doesn't work in practice.

Execution is always influenced by human factors, even if they are undesirable in yesterday's management. In Energetic Leadership, the rational approach is combined with not only recognising the human factor but also with gratitude for human contact and intuition. Execution takes place using a combination of professional and intuitive knowledge, with schedules that are a combination of fixed and flexible.

Good and efficient execution creates a good flow for everyone in the value chain and everyone in the organisation, with positive consequences for employee well-being. When everything runs smoothly, the energy is good, and everything is much more fun. Therefore, it is just as relevant to focus on the energy flow as on the process flow in an execution. Although it's quite logical, it's new in most organisations – and focusing on it can take execution and revenue to the next level.

On a managerial level, the questions could be:

- Is the way you execute up to date and keeping up with trends?
- Is there a budget allocated for an improved holistic execution, or might it even become cheaper?
- Are the people responsible for execution given speaking time in management?
- Are customers and employees regularly interviewed about how execution can be improved?
- Can silent listening be a relevant part of decision-making processes?

In management, it's also important to pay close attention to what constitutes magic moments.

- What gets customers and employees/managers high on energy, hands over their heads and smiling?
- Where has execution become an annoyance to customers and internally in the organisation?
- What makes managers afraid to allow employees to use their intuition when interacting with customers?
- What could be the reason employees ignore their intuition when interacting with customers?

Understanding execution with a content, process, and energy mindset and making room for intuition and inner creativity requires the ability to use the full range of your resources, your body, mind and soul.

When responsible for execution, you should ask yourself:

- Am I a role model for the company's execution?
- Am I allocating the time at work that is needed for me to be calibrated in my energy?

Unique balance

Life purpose

Life purpose relates to the person, i.e. the individual leader or employee. The personal life purpose should not be confused with the company's purpose.

The term has many names, and when it is personal, many refer to it more as my calling, my cause, my passion. Perhaps precisely to differentiate themselves from a corporate purpose (WHY).

But what's important to say here is that when you're employed, you need to think about whether your life purpose aligns with the company you work for. The 'conformist to rebel' trend speaks to the tsunami of people who have or are reevaluating their lives and work lives.

When it comes to life purpose, there is no right or wrong. The most important thing is that it becomes clear to you. It's a process, and it can't be rushed. It takes the time and years it needs. Some people find their passion early in life, others later. And that's okay. A life purpose can be adjusted over time.

A life purpose can create peace – inner and outer peace. And joy. It can happen quickly, like an explosion, or slowly. The process of finding your life purpose will initially be experienced as small flashes of light, impulses, and happiness in your body and mind that make you continue – and realise that this feels good and right. You return and do it again, and suddenly, you have a new habit, insight and behaviour that helps to open up the innermost part of your heart – your soul. The small flashes of light, coupled with persistence, guide you in the right direction, and suddenly, it all fits like the cogwheel falling into place. It feels so natural that no way back would make sense. Slowly – and sometimes with quick quantum leaps – you arrive in yourself, come home, and experience a strong inner joy and gratitude for experiencing this peace and meaning.

When individuals are at peace with themselves, it rubs off on the entire organisation. You bring it to work. It creates inner peace and meaning. It makes you unstoppable. Or you stop and find another way. It makes you realise that there can be something bigger than yourself. That your competencies are better used elsewhere.

In leadership, this means that you need to focus on whether there is a harmony between the employees' life purpose and the company's purpose, and in a way that doesn't just preach what you need to adopt, but where leaders curiously and exploratory support employees in their life purpose.

This could be through providing learning opportunities to help them along the way, through a human resources policy that allows for life breaks, or by allowing part-time work so the employee can also volunteer, work two jobs, or even run their own business.

Managers should ask themselves:

- What is the purpose of the organisation?
- Has the company strayed from its purpose?
- Do we know our employees' true driving force – their life purpose?
- In what ways are we helping employees pursue and live their life purpose?
- Are we communicating the company's purpose in a way that seeks to "convince" employees or in a way that invites trusting dialogue about their life purpose and how we can support them?

Of course, in personal leadership, you need to draw on your physical, mental, and spiritual competencies and talents and bring them all into play. But particularly, you should remember that the spiritual is the ultimate and most difficult piece. And that it's the one that makes it all come together.

Finding your life purpose takes time for most people. Finding and connecting with your soul can't be forced by brain power. Working on quieting down and listening to your body is a prerequisite. A quiet mind helps. Energy work, such as breathing and silence, is the path to the soul.

So the question to ask yourself is:

- Does the company's purpose align with my life purpose?
- Do I feel frustrated or annoyed by the way things are run, and is it a safe space for me to speak up?

- What are the best ways for me to calm my body and mind (nervous system)? Is it being in nature, being quiet, meditating, swimming, running, or weeding? When am I at my best, not with my head, but with my body?

The input you receive is worth its weight in gold!

☐ Note the observations you make when you are quiet and listen inwards (exercises at the back of the book).

Eventually, your life purpose will slowly emerge. It cannot be forced, and it should not be forced. It is part of the law of energy. Everything is as it should be.

We each have our path – a personalised path
Without pressure and competition
Trust and lean in

Meditation

Meditation helps and trains us to quiet the mind and listen to the body so we can better focus on "spiritual matters" like the soul. Meditation can be a pathway to the soul. It's a way to care for yourself by being in silence, listening, measuring and mediating between your inner and outer worlds.

The thing about meditation is:
You become more and more yourself
David Lynch[68]

The term meditation covers many different types of meditation. Unfortunately, there are also many misconceptions about meditation, so it may be necessary to explain what it actually is.

Meditation is a method for quieting the mind through focus, concentration and awareness. When we train the mind, we learn to be present.

Meditation is the modern term for a mental activity where the meditator mentally focuses on spiritual topics. Meditation is derived from the Latin meditor and meditatio, meaning "practise, prepare me for". [69] In Spanish, medir means to measure. In English, mediate means to negotiate common ground. You can, therefore, think of meditation as a conversation with our inner self in which we listen, measure and mediate the connection between our inner and outer selves.

It can be a guided meditation in which someone speaks to you, or it can be just you being quiet with yourself. You can have a mantra and say it until you find peace and drop yourself into your subconscious.

You could also say that mindfulness is in the meditation category. But the whole point is that it's about taking care of yourself, your body, mind, and soul by being quiet and going inward. It's not difficult, you can do it at any time of day and anywhere you want; outside, at home, and so on.

It's about awareness and connecting with the unconscious, which can help boost your creativity and intuition. It's a habit. And it can become a very healthy habit. Or you might forget about it and have to pick it up again. It's something that needs to be practised – both in terms of skill (how easy it is to reach the soul) and persistence (establishing and keeping a routine).

Meditation has a proven positive effect on our nervous system and our physique[70]. Meditation can help us reduce anxiety and stress, increase our sensation of happiness and focus, and improve our creativity and health.

Some people think meditation is dangerous or religious. It's not. It's completely harmless and has nothing to do with religion. It's about controlling your breathing, balancing your mind and nervous system, and finding calmness.

Meditation is a form of exercise because it trains the mind. It also indirectly trains the body, even if you're still, and it especially trains the soul.

Is it accepted? No, there are still many wrong beliefs and prejudices about it. But it is gaining ground everywhere and has, in Asian culture, been a natural part of personal leadership. The reason why meditation is being elevated as something unique and a form of exercise that is special and should be given some extra space is that it has such a beneficial effect on our health. India even has a ministry of holistic health, named the Ministry of Ayush, which focuses on education and research in Ayurveda, Yoga and Naturopathy, Unani, Siddha, and Homoeopathy.

There are many forms of meditation, so it's a matter of taste what you are attracted to.

Primordial sound meditation is based on repeating a mantra, such as "Ohm", over and over again. When you say this mantra, your mind becomes free of thoughts, taking you out of the present.

Vipassana (insight meditation) is based on nasal breathing and identifying thoughts and emotions without judgement.

Zazen meditation, also known as Zen, is based on belly breathing in a seated position. In it, you learn to recognise your thoughts and set them free.

Metta meditation is also called loving kindness and is based on Tibetan Buddhism. It is a caring and compassionate way of meditating that helps you clear your own beliefs and empathise with others.

Kundalini meditation awakens your mind by activating your spine and nervous system. This is done through mantras, chants, and exercises that access your unconscious mind. When you recite these mantras and chants, energy in your spine is released, allowing you to wake up and make better contact with yourself – your soul.

Chakra meditation has its roots in Hinduism. The meditation is done by focusing sounds, visualising and positioning your hands on the desired chakra area.

Tonglen meditation is a form of meditation that helps you connect to suffering and pain and liberate yourself from it.

Many people associate meditation with mental control and find it difficult to "empty" the mind, "think about nothing", and "concentrate on not being present". Luckily, it doesn't have to be that way.

Transcendental Meditation (TM) is about being yourself (transcending). This form is the most widely practised (six million practitioners) and the most well-documented (over 600 studies). Research indicates that it is the most relaxing technique. TM is easy because it is fundamentally different from many other mediation techniques. It doesn't require concentration and discipline.

TM was rediscovered 60 years ago when a young Indian physicist, Maharishi Mahesh Yogi, discovered that meditation is not about controlling the mind. He developed a method to teach people how to activate a natural process in which the mind, by itself, enters a state of inner stillness without effort.

I myself practise Transcendental Meditation by sitting for 20 minutes in the morning and evening in a relaxed position with my eyes closed, repeating my mantra. After a while, I am "gone" – transcended. I can resume the mantra if thoughts arise.

I also use some of the other forms of meditation. I try to listen to what my body and mind need. My main rule is that it should feel good. It doesn't work for me if, during my meditation, I have to think about what kind of thoughts I have, so I focus on breath and mantra, or breath, resetting and transcending.

My best recommendation is to try different forms and see what works for you. The most important thing in order to benefit from meditation is to make it a habit, just like sleeping and eating, and that's the hardest part.

Hopefully, it will become more accepted in society and therefore more natural, so that it's just something we do either alone or together – even in educational institutions and workplaces. Imagine how much time we spend in front of a TV. We just need to cut 20-40 minutes of screen time and spend it on self-love.

In professional leadership, it's important to realise that this is a form of exercise that can create peace, balance, and connection to the soul. There are at least three reasons why this is relevant to the workplace:

- It unlocks our intuition and creativity, making us better at running a business
- It creates better health and well-being and amazing self-care, reducing stress and increasing well-being
- It helps create better cohesion throughout society when nervous systems have calmed

A company or a management team can ask themselves:

- Does management understand what meditation is?
- Is it possible to meditate at work?
- Is it part of the people's policy?
- Does management do it themselves?

And in your personal leadership, you can increase your knowledge and skills by reading about meditation, practising breathing, practising mental and spiritual energy work, and talking to others about experiences with meditation.

Remember that personal development is personal. So it's not about looking at what and how your neighbour is doing. It's about looking only at your own "yoga mat".

You should:

- ☐ Try out different forms of meditation and find out which one suits you.
- ☐ Establish good meditation habits, like brushing your teeth.

Frequencies, sound healing and light language

The focal point of Energetic Leadership is energy, and as previously mentioned, as humans, we are energy and frequencies vibrating in a vast web. We have become increasingly aware of this, and to such an extent that we now dare to open up to using that part of ourselves.

> *If you want the secret of the Universe,*
> *think in terms of energy, frequency and vibration*
> **- Nikola Tesla**

This also means that we are opening up to using energy as a modality, a treatment method to help us with inner development and healing of body, mind and soul.

But what exactly are frequencies and resonance?

Frequency is the rate at which energy (flow) changes direction per second – also called the frequency of a tone or oscillation number, measured in hertz (Hz).

Resonance occurs when we are exposed to an impact with a frequency similar to our own frequency.

Our voice is a frequency that affects others. If the frequency is low, it sends low energy to the environment. If it's high, it sends high energy to the environment. In this way, we affect our surroundings negatively and positively. This is not really new information, but something we've known at a principal level. We tend to say – about an uncomfortable atmosphere in a room – that there is bad energy or bad chemistry among those present.

What's new is that some of our highly conscious fellow humans are blessed with the ability to channel sounds from the universe that tap into our frequency and heal by lifting us earthly beings out of our human density. These sounds are called light language or light codes and heal gently and subtly. They recode our energy by clearing karmic impints and trauma from our own lives or our lineage. Trauma that has settled as fear, grief, anger, etc.

The sounds, both as song (sound healing) and words (light language), work on the subconscious level and are the key to accessing our innermost being. The key to the soul. The sounds exit the person's mouth unhindered. Indeed, the person who has the ability and has made themselves available for channelling cannot help it; it happens automatically.

What comes out is not planned or known in advance, so they are not sounds or words that are recognisable to humans. The channelled sounds can also be supported by simple yoga-like exercises for the body. The sounds are a form of light language and soul singing. A session can last from 5 minutes to 1.5 hours and can be done in person or online. It can be for a group or an individual channelling for a specific person.

Sessions with sound healing and light language are a very enjoyable way to short-cut to find back to your soul faster and to "deal with" what needs to be dealt with on the way there. What that might be is completely personal and individual. It can be physical pain, imbalances or blockages that are removed in the process or afterwards.

Through frequencies (sound and words), you can work with your personal development and create greater joy, clarity, abundance and self-care so that your life purpose, strength and presence become the stable core of an ever-changing life, easily and without medication.

I have used sound healing and light language programmes [71] as part of my energy training to stay both healthy and well. It feels great on all levels to melt into the energy, feel the tingling sensation in the body of energy at work, and "cleanse" and calibrate the accumulated clutter. Significant parts of this book were "channelled" – or you could say it has come through my intuitive source – my soul – with the help of sound healing and light language.

It happens in a very, very enjoyable way; all you're doing is listening with your body. Not just with the brain in our head but with all our brains (head, heart and gut), in other words, with the whole body. The sounds and signals (frequencies) go directly into the cells, and they do what they are supposed to do without you having to think about it, but simply set the intention to receive.

This method can help save healthcare costs, both individually and at a societal level. Instead of taking aspirin or whatever treatments we receive, it can provide better healing and well-being for patients and carers. In the organisation, it can lead to fewer sick days, more and better motivation and innovation, greater job satisfaction, and thus better decisions.

For a management team that practises Energetic Leadership, it is natural to consider new training methods and treatment trends. It is obvious to lean on a practice that has produced good results for many years. [72]

Questions for management could be:

- Do you dare to try sound healing and let it be part of the workplace's offerings as prevention and personal development?
- How can healing sounds and tones be a strategic part of the company's work environment?
- IIow can healing sounds be a natural part of core deliverables and execution (behavioural design)?

In personal leadership, you can unlock some truly magical moments with an energising bath.

Ask yourself:

- Do I dare to trust my intuition?
- When do I dare and when don't I dare, and why?
- Am I giving myself enough self-care?
- What am I doing to develop my talents and potential?

CHAPTER 8

Energetic leadership with future-sense

Purpose

Purpose is a description of why the company was created and, thus, its reason for existence, as seen through the eyes of its creators. It is the rudder of the organisation. Most large organisations, foundations, and NGOs have a defined purpose. However, not all businesses have a purpose unless the owner started the company out of passion and has a goal beyond making money.

A purpose is non-negotiable, whereas goals can be adjusted. The purpose is the entire foundation of the business. It is the root of the thoughts, intentions, and dreams of the soul that gave birth to the business. It's the why first, followed by the what and how.

The purpose should be known by everyone, allowing everyone to be involved in pursuing it, being it, and ensuring the company stays on course.

That said, very few people actually know the purpose of the workplace they're a part of. Most employees hear about the goals, how much revenue, bottom line, and market share should increase and how it should happen. And in the eagerness to measure and communicate that, the link to the purpose is forgotten. Not only for customers and employees but also for management themselves, who lose sight of the purpose in the fog of everyday tasks.

In recent years, some purposes have been dusted off and added to the narrative, especially now that sustainability has become important. Other organisations have yet to articulate this and may not consider it crucial – but it is.

Purpose is not the same as vision and growth goals. The purpose should be known by management and the board, and they are the ones responsible for ensuring it lives.

A purpose can be articulated in all sorts of ways; there is no set format. A few examples are:

- To develop and produce sustainable products for industry X
- To find the cure for disease X
- To inspire and facilitate X to succeed with Y
- Providing clear, objective recommendations about X
- To help and support people and animals in need

Patagonia Inc. has put it this way:

> "At Patagonia, we appreciate that all life on earth is under threat of extinction. We're using the resources we have – our business, our investments, our voice and our imaginations – to do something about it. Earth is now our only shareholder."

For professional leadership, the purpose is the foundation of the narrative that must be conveyed to investors, customers, employees and suppliers in all communication, internally and externally, and on which the owners (the board) hold management accountable. It is also the foundation of values and principles and the basis for the culture to be created.

There are two questions a company can ask itself, especially in these times of significant change:

- What is the company's purpose?
- Has the company strayed from its purpose? And why?

You may have a great purpose, but perhaps you have become too profit-orientated and forgotten some of the original intent behind the company's creation, for example, due to changing management teams and disagreements about direction.

It becomes important to consider the original purpose, how things are being done right now, and how you expect employees' life purposes to evolve to create a kind of harmony where employees can be relevant and natural sources of inspiration so that together, you can create the workplace of the new era.

In personal leadership, leaders can look at whether their life purpose matches the purpose of the workplace or whether they are simply there because of norms, prestige, culture or other people's expectations.

Surprisingly, often, there is a mismatch between what you stand for and what the organisation is leading from. Do you, in reality, feel that there is no purpose? Or is there an unhealthy purpose that you find hard to support? Or has your life purpose, and therefore integrity, been run over?

Either way, it's important for you, and especially your organisation, to note the signals that are present. You may experience reactions in yourself that physically manifest themselves as otherwise unexplained pain in the body, mentally by having racing thoughts, and spiritually by the soul going AWOL if it's not a good place to be.

So the question to yourself, as a leader, might be:

- Are you experiencing frustration or meaninglessness in your work?
- If there are discords, what exactly is causing the disharmony between your life purpose and the company's purpose?
- What impact does the difference have on your work?
- Is your life purpose truly rooted in your soul?
- If you and the company are not a good fit, what will you do about it? How will you do it? And when?
- What would be (even) better in line with your life purpose?
- What do you need to dare to get there?

Strategy

A strategy is based on an organisation's purpose, values, vision, and mission. It is usually a long-term (5-10 years) plan and blueprint of what it takes to realise the purpose and vision – and to be the purpose.

The strategy contains what it takes to attract, develop and retain customers and employees, including how to work holistically, profitably and efficiently. The strategy translates into initiatives and activities that will help achieve the goals. It's all analysed, calculated, broken down into multi-year KPIs, and laid out in time and project plans with milestones linked to essential people's bonus agreements. Boom – we're ready to go.

Well, no. That's the "old" way of strategising. Going forward, in the new type of leadership, you can expect an even greater degree of intuitive leadership in terms of what the initiatives are; when they should happen; and how tightly you stick to linear timelines.

We've already had a taste of this during COVID-19, with several business leaders stating that it's impossible to plan anything, neither strategy nor budget. Hooray for good preparation for what will be the reality for many years to come, and which holds the only truth: Change (also in people's priorities and values) is the only constant factor we can count on.

A more adaptive form of leadership is and will be necessary. A softening of the fixed plan that we stick to "no matter what". In this way, Covid has been a bridge to a better and more intuitive approach, although none of us want to go back to that time, which has also seen far too many tragedies.

A strategy requires clear communication. It must be understood by everyone and created by more than just management. We all know this – and we also know that it's incredibly difficult to achieve. The old classic quote "culture eats strategy for breakfast" applies more than ever, as workplace culture is challenged in many ways, as mentioned in several trends in Chapter 2:

- We quit if we are not seen, heard, met and understood
- We quit if management is not proactive and driving impact
- We quit if we don't experience trust and respect
- We quit if there is no flexibility and self-management

The strategy and the process that creates it must be sustainable both internally and externally. Otherwise, we just don't want to be a part of it anymore. We're done unpleasantly paying our dues to be included and respected.

In leadership, strategy is a management tool that creates direction and that the board, if you have one, can hold the company up to.

A business leader can ask themselves:

- What will it take for the strategy to live up to having the planet as a shareholder?
- What does it take for the strategy to have dualism as its centre of gravity?
- What does it take for the strategy to be based on partnerships?
- What does it take to dare create a strategy based on a radical new business model?

In the personal leadership of those who work with the strategy in the company, they must become insanely good at reading the personal and energetic compass and work tirelessly to ensure that the strategies support a modern form of leadership with intuitive foresight – both in the content and the practice in which it unfolds.

On a personal level, you can help by being a test subject through your energy. It takes strong awareness to be able to listen and hear your sensations and act on them so that it's not your ego, bonus, salary, prestige, and pride that rule but your life purpose in harmony with the organisation's purpose.

You can ask yourself:

- What will it take for you to raise your energetic leadership level?
- How can you infect others with your energetic leadership?

Leadership

Leadership is about knowing your wisdom, knowledge, skills, and behaviours from the inside out – whether we're talking about business leadership, team leadership, or personal leadership.

While purpose is the rudder, leadership is the helmsman who steers the organisation in the desired direction, often in turbulent seas.

Leadership and management have evolved a lot over time, and we are on the threshold of a radically different style of leadership, moving from the very ego-driven and top-down style to a much more holistic and inclusive style that goes far beyond adding a few questions on the performance review and performance appraisal forms, and dedicating times for questions or a few hours of group work at the annual meeting.

Leadership must be embedded in both the organisation and management itself – daily. As a manager, you have accepted this responsibility as your most important task. You have been given power and influence for a period, and it must be managed with humility and care.

Leadership and time for leadership are constantly challenged by the focus and time spent on operational matters. This is where a leader would benefit from bringing their intuitive skills into play to help with just that. When management dares to believe that balanced intuitive leadership is healthier for all parties and will help to achieve better results on all bottom lines, a quantum leap is made:

- Better self-management and flexibility trigger joy and intuition.
- Better involvement and trust create less conflict and better and simpler processes.
- Better well-being and culture release blocked energy and create better results, both financially and in terms of satisfaction.

This is where, from now and into the future, we're going to see a serious shift for the better that will make management and leadership easy and sought-after again.

Professional leadership is about creating an exhilarating energy in a thriving incubator, with plenty of room to play and use your creativity and intuitive instincts. The world craves that.

There are four questions a manager or leader should ask themselves regarding leadership:

- What will it take for you to have the courage to grow into *being* the new leadership?

- What will it take for you to change your business model to the new leadership?
- What will it take for you to take each other to the next level?
- What will it take for your owners to see the "light" in the new leadership and business model?

In your personal leadership, you can embrace the new planetary way: to be still, feel, listen, and see. And most importantly, believe in what you sense. Because when you bring your full energetic potential into play, you can tap into your innermost being and create the foundation for abundant joy.

Ask yourself:

- What is the reason I have a leadership job?
- What will it take to elevate my energetic leadership?
- What is holding me back from taking action?
- Who are my energetic mentors?

Do the silent listening exercise (1) at the back of the book and establish good habits around regularly listening inwards and finding the answers within yourself.

"

You risk coming across as an idealist who is not commercially orientated.

*I get frustrated when capitalism rules over
our humanistic values.*

*Disruptions are not just going to come from technology like AI. They will
come from people demanding change.*

We've become more conscious. It has influenced me, how we treat our planet. I wouldn't have thought about that 10 years ago.

*I thought the only thing that would happen if I was really good at my job
was that the shareholders would get richer. The world wouldn't be a better
place.*

*I've become better at being aware of my own needs
and what I want.*

*I wish to see a world where people are compassionate towards each other
and where new ideas and technologies are developed through collaboration
to improve the quality of life for all.*

CHAPTER 9

Cases

SABRINA SULLIVAN, Futuring Strategist and Foresight Fellow at Ford Motor Company, US and Founder of by+by foresight, Canada.

What do you wish to see more of in the world?

In a world brimming with endless possibilities, I yearn for the resurgence of AUTHENTIC CURIOSITY, a profound eagerness to truly understand others and their perspectives. By fostering a deep sense of empathy, this kind of curiosity encourages us to connect on meaningful levels, recognising and appreciating where others come from. It's a pathway from a mindset of scarcity to one of abundance, inviting us to see beyond our differences and embrace the vast array of possibilities before us. Embracing authentic curiosity not only opens the door to learning and understanding but also paves the way for a more empathetic and united world.

What is good leadership to you?

Good leadership, to me, transcends the mere title or role we often attribute to those at the helm. It's not about having your ego validated or about the formal authority to manage tasks or teams. True leadership is earned through the recognition of others, bestowed upon those who inspire, guide, and elevate those around them. It's about enabling others to unlock their full potential, fostering an environment where they can become even greater leaders.

And, with that, the essence of leadership lies in its capacity to evolve. As we face a future filled with unprecedented challenges and disruptions, not only from advancements in AI but also from societal shifts, for example, our traditional notions of leadership are going to (if they haven't already) be put to the test. We must embrace new ways of leading – ones that challenge our conventional beliefs and practices.

The leaders of tomorrow will be those who dare to think differently and who are willing to redefine what it means to lead in an era of constant change and uncertainty.

Leadership, therefore, is about adaptability, innovation, and the courage to pave new paths. It involves questioning and reimagining our approaches in light of the complex issues we face, both within and beyond our organizational walls. As we navigate through these times of 'permacrisis,' it becomes clear that leadership is less about control and more about the ability to steer through chaos with vision and resilience. Ultimately, it's about creating a legacy of empowerment, preparing the ground for future leaders to thrive in a world that is constantly evolving.

What do you see as the challenge for business leadership right now?

One of the primary challenges I observe in business leadership today hinges on courage – the boldness to look ahead, particularly when it might challenge the immediate or requires you to balance the short and long term. Our prevailing systems reward short-term gains, overshadowing the strategic value of flexibility and long-term planning. This scenario necessitates a shift towards foresightful leadership (a concept that I and a collaborator in industrial organisational psychology have distilled), where curiosity and the ability to envision a better future play pivotal roles. Leaders must wrestle with the dilemma of driving toward a preferred future while feeling increasingly powerless to do so, often hindered by a lack of boldness. But with this, what we have to grapple with as leaders is how do we start to communicate and drive towards a preferred future as leaders when we feel that we might have less and less control over doing that or we do not have that sort of courage to do it?

The path to overcoming these obstacles is steeped in elements like introspection, a task that becomes formidable without inherent self-awareness of yourself as a leader. Acknowledging one's limitations or biases is a challenging process. You must dedicate time to uncover hidden aspects of yourself. Most sessions I've driven around leadership become something akin to therapy because we have to build this awareness to know and start to uncover what we can do.

We must find ways to cultivate a sense of psychological safety that permits leaders to present themselves authentically and without fear. The feedback I receive from sessions where we dedicate pause and thought to self-awareness points to the uniqueness of this experience. (What I hear is that they aren't getting this somewhere else.) It underscores the necessity of granting leaders the freedom to redefine their approach and show up as themselves (and differently). Embracing this vulnerability, leaders can foster innovation and resilience, essential qualities for navigating the complexities of today's business environment within themselves, and hopefully extend that to their teams.

Do you see any differences in leadership from country to country?

Yes, every place has its own culture. Its norms, its orthodoxies, and the unspoken assumptions we hold today that shape us as leaders and the systems and structures leaders must operate in.

Also, the experiences that shaped our values are critical to think about, too, and differ between generations and countries.

I believe values are the hardest things to change or shift, and even though they manifest differently depending on the context (e.g., environments they work in and disruptions they face), they play a large part in how people act and show up.

What role does foresight play in business leadership?

Foresight is increasingly recognised as a crucial competency for effective leadership, as gleaned from conversations with seasoned leaders and through dedicated study. Foresightful Leadership™ demands the integration of positive vision and purposeful action, characterised by several key attributes such as:

- Challenging the status quo as a helpful provocateur while honouring valuable lessons from the past.
- Welcoming diverse perspectives to fuel necessary change
- Acknowledging the discomfort that often precedes transformation.
- Acting as a visionary – crafting and communicating a future that inspires positive action, and exemplifying innovative leadership.

Recent surveys reveal a concerning trend: 40% of CEOs fear their businesses may not survive the next five years. This anxiety underscores a widespread deficiency in foresight – many leaders struggle to anticipate future challenges and shape their strategies accordingly. The traditional separation between foresight and strategy has led to a reactionary approach, overly focused on short-term planning and budget management.

However, the advent of strategic foresight, which incorporates an abundance of both qualitative and quantitative data, offers a new path forward. Despite the overwhelming influx of information, or "infobesity," which often paralyses decision-making, leaders must learn to navigate this landscape with confidence. Bold decisions and experiments become feasible when leaders understand how to sift through data to find what's truly relevant for long-term visioning and transformative change. Foresight involves recognising the inherent uncertainty beyond the immediate future and preparing to lead creatively and innovatively, instilling confidence in teams even when complete information is elusive.

Looking ahead, I foresee a rise in leaders who embrace foresight, asking profound questions and seeking deeper insights into their decision-making processes. These Foresightful Leaders understand the significance of this crossroads and are committed to exploring and addressing the complex challenges that lie ahead.

Do you think humans are connected?

Absolutely, humans are inherently connected. The profound sense of loss we feel when isolated or disconnected underscores our natural interconnectedness. Our very essence is tied to our relationships with others, revealing a universal bond that unites us all. Show me one person who can do it all on their own!

MARLENE RAU, former Head of Marketing and Communication at SOS International. Marlene has a career in marketing and communication.

What does the future of leadership look like?

We will probably be more and more driven by purpose. Tasks and topics must make sense to people. Maybe we will work more freelance-based in a more dynamic society in the future! This means we need to become better at onboarding people and faster to create value.

I don't think leadership will get easier in more dynamic environments, as some people do fine with unclear roles while others need more clarity. A dilemma could be that we end up with a zapper culture, where people move on to the next job faster and don't stay and work for long-term purposes. I don't know if this will be the case, but we are probably less loyal to workplaces than before.

SOS International focuses on employee well-being and employee engagement. My reflection is that at SOS International, where our core service is to help people in critical and distressing situations, we attract people with empathy who are executors and make a difference. For example, you must not become part of the client's emotions but be empathetic, understand their feelings and the situation, and make concrete decisions that can help the person in an unfortunate situation.

Why are we unhappy in organisations?

Well, unfortunately, it's not just in organisations. It's in society that there is unhappiness. I want to take it to a completely different place. Where I'm probably most concerned right now is: how do we define well-being? Are the lives we live aligned with what we want?

I have a scepticism towards KPIs and the performance culture because it has a side effect: it creates demand for the standardisation of people. That is sad. We have to constantly optimise, run on the margins, slim down the organisation – and we've done this at a time when society and the financial situation were in growth with very low inflation and peacetime. Does that create engagement and well-being?

For me, it's our understanding of society that we need to question. Is optimisation the way to prosperity, well-being, and engagement?

What triggers you?

Do we dare to talk about our concerns in the management room? It depends on the culture you are part of. You risk appearing as an idealist who is not commercially orientated. Here at SOS International, we can discuss values, relationships and different personality types.

I get frustrated when capitalism rules over our humanistic values. It didn't have to be that way. We could make diversity an advantage, but there is a tough road ahead.

Discussion on sustainability

We discussed sustainability in our management group. Is it because we want to be sustainable or because it's a good business idea? I guess most sustainability initiatives come about and receive approval because it's good business. Ideally, we want to be sustainable, but initiatives also have to be financially viable. I guess that's probably why development is slow. Most often, there needs to be a business idea and business value before we actually work with sustainability.

JESPER BRAM is a digital futurist, an innovation facilitator at energy company Andel DI, and the founder of Online Change Makers.

What is your take on new leadership?

Slowing down has become a mantra for me. It starts with being able to lead yourself. Figure out who you are, what you want and why. For me, narrow-minded and rebellious as I am, I have finally accepted that my reality is my reality. I believe mostly in my inner self. Some believe in external signals. I can feel it in my state of being. I can feel my intuition. I can remember from my intuition. I can feel the direction I need to go. I remember it from when I was a boy. I have often experienced that the first thing is the first choice. I've learnt a lot about myself and that it's important to practise, not just think. At some point, I came up with a principle I call STFD – Slow The Fuck Down. I have to remind myself of this every once in a while so I don't just blast off but remember to be where I am and enjoy it. I would like there to be a greater sense of community. Someone is supposed to try to change that.

How have you taken responsibility for your personal leadership?

I've developed my method involuntarily over 25 years – run until I hit the wall – learn and change direction, and then run again. Many times, I've ignored the advice and paid the price – "Failing your way forward", as Tim Ferris says. From the age of 16 to my mid-30s, I didn't listen to anyone. I guess I've always seen myself as someone who had to create something. More than I've seen myself as an employee in the classic sense.

I've been drawing since I was a kid. So, for many years, I thought I was going to work with graphics. I started at one of Denmark's first web agencies in the late 90s, where we helped create Midas for Saxo Bank and build their first digital platform. This led me on a long journey into tech startups over many years. My approach was to hammer through and hit the wall over and over again.

What changed that was something I heard somewhere: "What got you here won't get you there". That was new to me – it made me wonder if I should do something completely different. Maybe it wasn't the hands-on, creative craftsmanship that interested me the most. I had achieved what I needed to. Working with big brands and being published in books and magazines all over the world. Perhaps it was really the creativity of strategic leadership that I had learned to appreciate.

At one point, I was teaching both online and in person. It forced me to figure out the psychology of how to teach. It led me down a rabbit hole about how we function as humans – and how we can evolve. I believe that the more we grow ourselves, the more our business grows – "Progress beyond what you currently believe is possible" is another quote I find quite interesting in this context.

PER GRAABÆK VENTZEL - Head of Audit, Chief Audit Executive at ATP – a pension fund.

What is inner sustainability?

I believe that as humans, we need to challenge ourselves and ask ourselves the question "Why am I here and can I reflect myself in the values and the environment I am a part of?". If the 'why' gets a little blurry, there's every reason to reconsider your situation.

In my case, it was an opt-in to ATP, which is largely due to ATP's unique role in the Danish welfare society. Having the opportunity to work for the benefit of the welfare society in Denmark and help ATP ensure the basic financial security in Denmark is in line with my inner sustainability.

As Head of Audit at ATP, my and the team's primary task is to reassure management about the effectiveness of the governance and risk management system and the internal control processes. We look beyond financial risks and consider issues such as reputation, growth, environment, and social impact. This has had a big impact on my personal choice of ATP.

In the past, I was probably less concerned with inner sustainability. It's definitely something that has increased in recent years. I also find that reputation, growth, the environment and the social aspect are far more important today than in the past, for example in connection with recruitment – especially for younger candidates.

What has changed for you?

There may be some correlation with Maslow's Hierarchy of Needs. As human beings, I think most of us develop our outlook on life over time and maybe even reach a point where we want to self-actualise. At my age, my basic needs are fulfilled, and I view the world through a different lens than in my younger years.

There are certain values that I value more today than in the past. For example, there are jobs or sectors that I would exclude today due to incompatibility with my values. When I entered the labour market (in the mid-1990s), it wasn't something that necessarily had the same importance.

I think as a society we've become much more conscious of things like sustainability. It has influenced me in terms of how we treat our planet. I wouldn't have thought about that 10 years ago.

What would you like to see more of in the world?

Trust. The courage to trust your leaders and dare to lead in a new way. Sustainable trust is difficult and context-dependent. An example is the financial sector, where trust was shattered after the 2008 financial crisis.

Being courageous and daring to make the difficult decisions to restore trust is precisely what leadership is all about. We must do it in a sensible and balanced way. The most important raw material is people, and developing competencies is the best investment we can make.

How do we help leaders develop more future-oriented competencies?

The understanding of what the role of a leader entails is changing. Future generations, including those coming through the education system, will challenge the existing way of "being" led. As leaders, we need to stop seeing ourselves as superiors. We need to redefine what the role of a leader is.

To lead is to set the direction and execute the strategy together in a trusting way. Believing that you, as a leader, know everything and decide everything is wrong and does not create sustainable leadership.

NATJA AABERG HORNSBÆK - HR Director at Elis – a laundry business.

How do you work with culture?

What I think is amazing about Elis is that what you say is what you do. Values are not just something that's written on the wall. It's really part of the DNA. There's a huge pride and dedication to what we do.

I came in and saw it all very much from a development & leadership perspective but was met with operations and green or red metrics. And so I asked, "Don't we have a common attitude towards management?" So, we started by identifying our Leadership DNA in the executive board for use in the strategy process.

Then, we created the strategy based on a circular model and added resources to CSR and HR, sending a signal to the organisation, which could suddenly see and feel that we do what we say. We redefined our leadership development based on how we see the future of leadership and decided on the following six soft competencies: appreciative, empathetic, curious, holistic, proactive, and persistent, as well as some hard competencies.

We created a leadership programme with 3 modules: 1) Lead yourself, 2) Lead others, and 3) Structure and planning, where everything is built on trust. The last module became a necessity as we were aware that to ensure time for leadership, you need to be able to prioritise and organise your time.

It has been a big and positive change for our culture, where we focus on local needs, silence in meetings, 1:1 conversations, and difficult conversations – being able to talk and understand each other and remembering to recognise each other for small and big things.

How do you look after yourself?

I used to think I was very extroverted and always found energy through people. I've realised over time that it's really important for me to have my own time and just be myself. It's also important for me to be curious and develop myself. Listening to podcasts, going to the theatre, and talking to my boyfriend energises me. I need to be challenged and inspired by others.

JOHANNA KIEL NIELSEN - CEO and Founder of Børneloppen – a franchise chain for second-hand children's clothes and toys.

What is your WHY?

I was in a "regular" job and asked myself, "If I'm really good at my job, what does it contribute to this company? How does that make the world a better place?" The shareholders get richer; that's what's going to happen. I thought, "That's not good enough, Johanna! You can do it better!"

I needed to do something more concrete than selling insurance policies. And so Børneloppen was born. We use a business model we knew worked well in Finland (Johanna is Finnish). We can do something good for the environment, and we can do something we find fun, namely the short time from idea to action as an entrepreneur in retail. I wanted to fulfil my dream, and I have done that.

How do you create a great culture?

That's the million-dollar question. That we have good values with a good tone of voice, and that we are personal and present. In Børneloppen, you can almost be allowed to do anything if you have a good idea. We need to be better at celebrating successes though.

How do you maintain your inner sustainability?

I've become better at being aware of my own needs and what I want. Self-love in a good way. At home, I enjoy turning on the sauna and being alone while the family watches a movie. It's nice and quiet.

Are we humans connected?

We are in different constellations with each other. At the workplace, in the local community, in our country, and in the world. I really try to understand what's happening in the world right now, and I listen and talk in a Twitter space where many different people bring up topics. What we have in common is that we are critical and want to understand the complex world better and gain a more nuanced insight into what's going on.

CHRYSTI LUCKYNELLY - Co-founder and Chief Marketing Officer of The Self Hug – a company focusing on human well-being.

What would you like to see more of in the world?

I want to see more inclusivity, kindness, and innovation. In today's fast-paced and competitive world, it can be easy to become overly focused on success and achievements, which can take a toll on our mental and emotional health. We neglect what is very important for all of us: happiness and well-being. I wish to see a world where everyone – individuals or organisations – treat each other (or their employees) fairly and with respect, where people are compassionate towards each other, and where new ideas and technologies are developed through collaboration to improve the quality of life for all.

How would you describe the future Leadership?

What I appreciate about today's leadership is that it is now less about a top-down approach where people are given instructions to follow immediately. Today, it's more about setting a positive example for the team to follow, providing direction and support, and empowering team members to take ownership of their work and contribute to the overall success of the company.

I observe that great leaders are the ones who are open to listening and considering other perspectives. Each individual is unique and can bring new perspectives, skills, and ideas that can help them and the company grow.

Some of the challenges include creating a sense of courage, trust, safety, and openness to discussions, which can help build a sense of belonging and resilience mentality in the team.

What has been your game-changer?

In 2020, like many others, I experienced mental struggles such as anxiety because of significant behavioural shifts in our daily routine, affecting the way we live, work, and socialise with one another. This is why my partner Kanina Priatna and I founded The Self Hug, which is an Indonesian wellness start-up with a mission to "Help young adults build sustainable healthy habits through simple and accessible science-backed wellness tools".

The pandemic was a wake-up call for many of us – individuals and companies. How we see mental health and the importance of well-being in the workplace became obvious. It highlighted the necessity for the growth of mental well-being, products, and services. However, the stigma surrounding mental well-being topics is still relatively strong, and it is our homework to educate people about mental well-being and how wellness tools like our guided journals help to improve their lifestyles and lead to healthier and happier lives.

.

Good habits

Good habits are good energy. They make for a good life. They make for a healthy body, mind and soul. But we're notoriously bad at sticking to them for very long.

With Energetic Leadership, habits come from a genuine intention rooted in the soul, making them functional in that cool way where they practically perform themselves. Because we become unstoppable when our actions are aligned with our soul.

We can't help but:

- Walking in unison with our breath
- Having quiet time every day
- Listening and acting on what our body tells us
- Eating healthy – or healthier
- Prioritising sleep
- Exercising physically, mentally and spiritually

Because we have embraced the 5 energetic principles:

- Set the pace of the day according to your energy
- Reset your energy several times a day
- Practise your energy awareness daily
- Ask and let your intuition guide you
- Be grateful

We actually think it's fun because learning and understanding the language of energy and having conversations with your body has become a sport. And it's liberating that we each have our path to well-being, so the old one-size-fits-all approach is history. And we love to connect and discuss with each other how we can improve.

As mentioned, change competence lies in both the horizontal and vertical development of the Energetic Leadership Model and always has three learning stages:

- **Technique** (which is what you need to do)
- **Method** (which is how you will do it)
- **Persistence** (which is the routine with which you will implement)

Now that you're wearing your intention-training outfit and soul-running shoes, here are some examples of how you can define the three steps for an area where you identify a need for change in behaviours.

For example, you might want to sleep eight hours, go for a walk in nature, or sit still and listen inwardly. That's the **technique**. This example links to the trend of moving from external sustainability to internal sustainability first, putting yourself first through mindset, health and balance to create outer balance in organisations, societies and nature.

The **method** is then how we make it our own. It could be sleeping in a cool room. Going for a walk in the woods in the rain. Being quiet and listening inwards while sitting in the train compartment.

For most people, **persistence** is the hardest part, which is why it's so important to consider if we want to be change-savvy and unstoppable so that we succeed in what we set out to do.

In the examples above, persistence could be sleeping eight hours every day from 10 PM to 6 AM. Going for a walk in nature every day when you get home from work. Being quiet and listening inwardly every day during the last 5 minutes of your lunch break. Or checking in with a friend every day for a period of time to stay on track.

In the new leadership, good habits become easier because they come from a genuine consciousness of wanting them because we can feel that it feels good and helps us in our lives and our leadership.

In professional leadership, good habits help create a good culture, good results, joy, well-being, collaboration and creativity. Good habits are, therefore, an important strategic and tactical tool in a leader's toolbox.

Leaders can ask themselves:

- How are good habits anchored in the strategy?
- What good habits does the company have, and are they part of its culture, values, and principles?
- Are employees involved, and do they have a say in creating good habits in the organisation?

As a leader, you can focus on:

- What comes easy to you (and energises you)?
- What do you find difficult (draining your energy)?
- In which areas would you like to create better habits?
- How do you best bring your entire zone of genius into play; your talents, your personality, your values, your professional and personal life experience, and your passion/life purpose?

The true potential

We all want to succeed in life, work and business. My vision is to bring out the full potential in people and businesses by connecting the commercial (business) sense with the energetic (human) sense. Our energetic future-sense.

When the leaders interviewed in the book and audiences at talks I've given were asked, "What would you like to see more of in the world?" the answer was usually prompt and often with just one word. Some hesitated a little as if asking themselves if they dared to say it out loud or if they needed to wrap it in more harmless words.

Although the words were diverse, there was a clear common thread. We need a new way of leading based on our true potential rather than rigid systems and outdated and unrealistic views of what employees want and can do today. A leadership style that celebrates respect, compassion, peace, time, accountability, trust, joy, love, genuine curiosity, inclusion, kindness, innovation, dialogue, and highly skilled people in a context where they have a chance to succeed, not only with the company's goals but with their individual life purposes.

As humans, we know what we want more of, to succeed and live the life we want. We can see it in our surroundings. We can feel it in our bodies, in what we are conscious of. But we have a harder time understanding and focusing on what our body is telling us. We don't quite dare to believe what our body, mind and soul are trying to tell us. We are comfortable with what we know, even if it hurts, is uncomfortable, and unsatisfactory, and we are insecure about our steps towards what we are attracted to. We miss the hand behind our backs.

Many companies are in the process of addressing the 17 SDGs and ESG reporting. But even though they are fine and very specific and concrete, they are mostly external global goals with associated accounting. The same goes for the futurology institutes, whose megatrends are still very much focused on the external world.

> *Be the change you want to see in the world, both in yourself, your country and also in the world.*
>
> **- Gandi**

This book is written as a call to action for companies and leaders who can do so much more for our planet and human well-being.

And it's written for those of you who miss more magical moments. Who miss your life and long for meaning, light and community. In your private life, at work, or both. You need to tap into the frustration, uncertainty, pride, prestige, passion, calling, joy, longing, and a lot more.

You long to find and hear your inner voice. The voice that can ignite your passion and raise your awareness of what's holding you back so you can shut down the self-criticism and prejudices about others and the opportunities you're afraid to seize or create. The awareness that allows you to set an intention for the way forward that is based on wisdom and not just knowledge.

We want trust, joy, compassion, time, peace, respect, inclusion, diversity, and accountability on the menu, and we know in our heads that we can achieve this. But how? We must learn to understand what the menu should consist of and how to create it. The good news is that it's not a complicated and time-consuming gourmet dish but a simple dish with basic ingredients and kitchen tools that we all know how to use.

You need to know that you've already passed the test. You are exactly what you need to be, and you already have everything you need. You just need to learn how to use it better. But that doesn't mean you should ignore the feeling that something is missing in your life, that you could contribute more or be healthier.

With this book, you get a lot of insight. You get physical, mental and spiritual training. You get professional training for your role as a person and as a leader. Hopefully, you find that the book piques your curiosity, rubs your frustration, challenges your irritation, releases your joy, and helps you set the intention. Not for the perfect life, but for true life.

Your true life.

As a leader, you, too, need to change. We need energy-aware leaders with the courage to recognise that the old model doesn't work. Leaders who acknowledge that leadership development for decades has primarily consisted of superficial buzzwords that have not addressed the root of the problem, that we do not have a common long-term interest in a healthy planet with healthy and happy people as the focal point of our activities and our use of skills. And that the younger generations, in particular – but also the older ones – will increasingly refuse to participate if we don't change direction.

Experienced leaders must be brave enough to raise their awareness to meet the currents that are – still often invisibly – bubbling just below the surface of the organisation (and the market) and that will soon break through the surface like an unstoppable geyser. And while new generations may be seen as part of the challenge by experienced leaders, it is exactly them who already have the DNA to walk their own paths and start new businesses that are more aligned with their life purpose.

Leaders must also be brave enough to recognise that they are not using their intuitive powers enough on the job, let alone making room for them in the organisation. The good news is that they, along with the organisation, hold the key to modern, intuitive foresight and the unlocking of true potential through new leadership styles, structures and business models. They can be the gift to lead us to a new path.

In collaboration with employees, leaders can develop and fulfil the 18th Sustainable Development Goal, which is missing from the UN list. There is a missing goal concerning inner, human sustainability, which also corresponds to the missing 16th megatrend, energetic understanding.

There is no need to wait for various formal institutions. We can do this by believing in what the energy and soul are already asking us to do, choosing to change direction and acting on what intuition and wisdom have been crying out for a long time. We can take control of our own lives and businesses. Today.

This book has come from within. It wasn't written from my head and has taken the time my soul asked for. It wasn't written because I had to tick something off a bucket list. It was written because it is something bigger than myself. It's my contribution to a better world.

It's my contribution to pushing us to realise that it is actually possible to make a brand new beginning with trust, joy and respect, which is much more enjoyable and allows us to experience that we have more – and better – time when we work smarter, not harder. This happens when we dare lean into an energy completely different from when fear is dominant. An energy that expands when we dare to trust ourselves, each other, and our own strong skills.

Our individual, personal path, which is not a copy of everyone else's path, but our own unique path to shine in a world that really needs people who thirst for lots of magical moments, lots of joy as we experience turbulent times, on the bridge to a better world.

As humans, we have everything we need. We have our gift, as Einstein said. We just need to learn how to find it. It's a powerful force, inspirer, and guide – our intuitive awareness. Then our rational servant, our head, our ego can follow along, smiling and whistling – and allow ego and soul to dance a close Argentine tango.

We have what we need to succeed at our fingertips – and with common sense and good habits, we can reach into the future.

I hope the book and the exercises inspire you and light up every space in you and the workplace.

Start practising and inspire change!

Gitte Madelaire

Exercises

All the exercises in the book are collected and presented below, so you have them all in one place, easy to find until they become a natural part of your daily routine. The exercises are for everyone, but if you already have or experience severe pain or other alarming discomfort along the way, you should, of course, consult a doctor.

1: Silent listening

Find a place where you can be by yourself – indoors or outdoors. This can also be a moment in your office chair or stopping in the corridor or street.

- Be quiet and still.
- Close your eyes if you feel like it.
- Listen and let your thoughts pass by.
- Feel your body and your energy.
- Do this for 1 minute, 10 minutes or 1 hour – as needed.

2: Gratitude and intention

Before you fall asleep or before you get up and out of bed.

- Spend a few minutes just lying there, quietly, with your eyes closed.
- Feel the energy in your body.

- Be grateful for what comes to you.
- Set your intention for the (next) day.
- Feel free to repeat it every night and morning.
- Notice if it affects your sleep and day.

3: Reset your energy

Find a place where you can just be by yourself.

- Shut out your surroundings and close your eyes if you feel like it.
- Focus your attention on yourself and your body.
- Focus on one sense at a time, e.g. hearing.
- When you keep focus on what you hear and feel calm, add one more, e.g. the sense of sight.
- You continue until you lose focus as your thoughts and attention get hold of you.
- Notice whether you can hold 2 senses or 3 or 5 and why that is. Sometimes it's less, and sometimes it's more. There is no right number.

4: Crunch in the body

If you're a little more experienced (you already know exercises 1 and 3), this exercise can be good if you need to get rid of the crunch (often emotional or physical) that you can feel in your body as discomfort, tingling or mild pain.

1. Reset your energy (see exercise 3 above).
2. Sit consciously, focusing on the discomfort.

3. Place your hands on your legs, palms facing up.
4. Set the intention to want to loosen it up.
5. Feel where it is in your body.
6. Focus on it.
7. Breathe deeply.
8. Direct, in your thoughts, energy to the discomfort.
9. Sit/be in the discomfort.
10. Continue to breathe slowly and calmly all the way down into your belly.
11. Feel that it hopefully eases.
12. Feel the energy in your body and how it feels.
13. Repeat as needed – but not on the same day

5: Minus Breathing (calmness)

Minus Breathing[73] is a great breathing exercise if you need to calm down during the day or after work. It draws oxygenation out of the blood.

- You breathe in and bring your breath and energy up to your head (figuratively speaking).
- Exhale through your nose all the way down through your body.
- The exhale should be longer than the inhale.
- After exhaling, pause for as long as you can and inhale again.
- You repeat it several times.
- If you feel you have toxins in your body that you want to get rid of, exhale through your mouth; otherwise, exhale through your nose.

6: Plus Breathing (energy)

Plus Breathing[74] is a great breathing exercise in the morning as it energises by oxygenating the blood. Spice it up with a positive mindset and you'll be off to a great start.

- You breathe in by breathing up through your body.
- When the inhalation and energy reach the top of your head, hold your breath for as long as you can.
- Then exhale through your entire body, all the way down to your toes, so that all the cells are happy.
- Exhaling should last longer than breathing in.
- You repeat this several times.
- If you feel you have toxins you want to get rid of, you should exhale through your mouth; otherwise, exhale through your nose.

7: Meditations

If you're new to meditation, I suggest you read the Meditation section (again) and feel which of the different meditations appeals to you.

Then, go on YouTube and give it a try. Alternatively, talk to someone in your social circle about what they do. You are also welcome to contact me at gitte@energeticleadership.eu.

Or try this relaxing meditation:

- Sit with your feet on the floor – the ground.
- Tap your feet slightly to energise them.
- Feel all 4 corners of your feet.
- Close your eyes.

- Breathe 3 times in through your nose and out through your mouth.
- Set the intention to receive.
- Sit for 20 minutes (you may want to set your alarm).
- Place your palms on your thighs to strengthen your grounding.
- If a thought comes, let it pass.
- Sit, breathe and be – you may be gone for a moment. If you fall asleep, it's because your body needs it.
- After 20 minutes, sit quietly for 2-3 minutes with your eyes closed and come back to the practical reality.
- Open your eyes and thank yourself for your time for self-care.
- It can be repeated daily.

8: Sound healing and light language

Sound healing, with its soft and gentle sounds, is a great way to repair all the tangled knots in our body and mind. So is light language, with its incomprehensible but penetrating soul language. Both can help simultaneously, or separately by simply lying down or sitting comfortably and receiving.

I recommend looking for more information in the following places:

Kathrine Krake
On Kathrine Krake's website, you can explore sound healing and light language and sign up for programmes and 1:1s.
https://www.kathrinekrake.com/

Sound Healing
Here, you find everything you need in sound healing, from a research foundation, education and programmes, therapy and treatment, and a webshop.

https://soundhealingcenter.com/

Light language – books and magazines

Patricia Walls: Unlocking the mysteries of Light Language
https://www.patriciawalls.net/

Yvonne M. Perry: Light language Emerging
https://www.amazon.com/Light-Language-Emerging-Activating-Integrating/dp/098906882X

Leslee Wegleitner: Light language – Harmonics of the Universe
https://www.edgemagazine.net/2023/02/light-language-harmonics-of-the-universe/

9: Train yes/no from ego and soul

Over time, it will become natural to consult your intuition more actively, and it will be useful to understand how your body expresses a yes from the ego (head) and from the soul (heart), and a no from the ego and soul.

- Sit comfortably and upright with your feet on the floor/ground.
- Place your hands on your legs, palms facing up.
- Do a reset – see number 3.
- Set the intention to get the answer that is in your best interest.
- Ask how a Yes from the soul feels – notice your body's reaction. This is your Yes from the soul.
- Ask what a Yes from the ego feels like – notice your body's reaction. This is your Yes from the ego.

- Ask how a No from the soul feels like – notice your body's reaction. This is your No from the soul.
- Ask what a No from the ego feels like – notice the body's reaction. This is your No from the ego.
- Your body's Yes and No from the soul and ego is what you should use in the future when you ask for advice. It's important to recognise your body's signals, so you know whether you are intuitively present and getting answers from the soul or the ego. If it's from the ego, you should pay extra attention and try to hear the soul.

10: Annoyance and indignation

When we want to learn to understand our patterns of thoughts, feelings, and beliefs, and thus our behaviour, this exercise can be very useful.

The exercise allows us to create better relationships by releasing the energy that blocks us through our automatic reactions. It is important to distinguish between irritation and indignation.

If you get **annoyed**, it's often a sign that you have some behaviour you need to adjust. When we are triggered by something or someone and become irritated, it is often about something we recognise as inappropriate in our behaviour. We can choose two paths: to go up (decide to go with the evolving mindset) and be interested and curious. Or we can choose to go down and be closed and judgemental.

I encourage you to welcome the annoyance because a lot of positive development is hiding in it.

- Notice when you get annoyed and why.

- Take the knowledge you gain from reflecting on the situation and feed it back to your behaviour.
- Experiment in your mind to do better the next time you encounter something similar. What should you do differently?

Example: A colleague tells you that you talk too much in the meeting and don't let others have their say. This is said constructively and helps you and the team, even though you might take it personally. At the next meeting, you'll be aware of it and let others have their say, too.

If you become **indignant**, it means that someone has crossed your boundaries and your moral and ethical values.

You can react by getting angry and expressing your frustration, or you can set the boundaries by speaking up in a friendly way.

- Recognise when you become indignant, why and how you react.
- Take the knowledge you gain from reflecting on the situation and feed it back into your behaviour.
- Experiment in your mind to do better the next time you encounter something similar. Is there anything you would do differently?

Example: Someone speaks very unkindly and unpleasantly to you in front of others. You either go up by expressing on the spot or later that you don't want to be spoken to like that. Or you go down by not saying anything. Your boundaries are unclear, and you're letting the person take up space in an unhealthy way that can cause stress.

11: Confused and clueless

If it's one of those days when you can't make sense of anything, look at the list below and feel into your body (energy) for what you need.

Choose one or more of these energy snacks, depending on your specific needs:

Increase feelings of satisfaction (increase dopamine)

- Complete a task
- Celebrate a success
- Self-care activities, e.g. exercises 1-10
- Eating and drinking

Increase feelings of joy and happiness (increase oxytocin)

- Playing with baby, children, friend, partner and animals
- Holding hands
- Complementing, singing, playing music
- Hugging family and friends

Stabilise mood (increase serotonin)

- Walk in nature – preferably barefoot
- Running, cycling, swimming, playing ball
- Being in the sunshine
- Meditate

Relieve pain (increase endorphins)

- Energy exercise (1-4), sound healing, light language
- Exercise and sleep
- Eat chocolate, listen to music
- Dance, laugh, watch a comedy

ABOUT THE AUTHOR

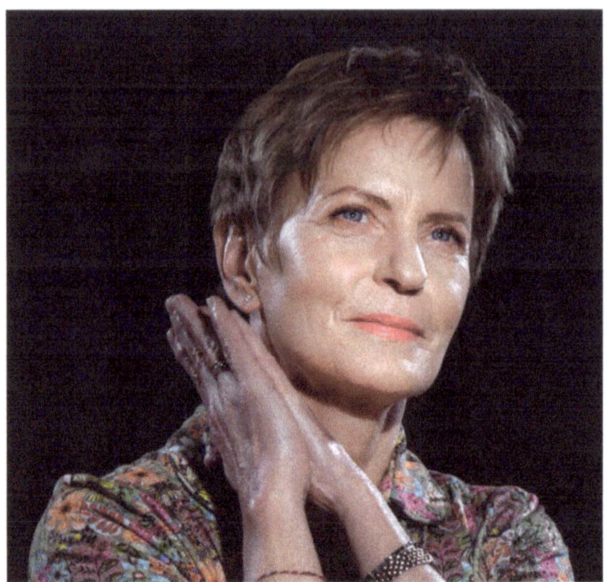

Photographer: *Marina Ozerova*
http://www.100portraits.hedonistphoto.dk/

Gitte Madelaire is an intuitive and visionary pioneer in leadership development. People, customers, business development, and futurism have always interested and motivated her. That we succeed individually and together. That we are better tomorrow than today.

With a background in corporate business at companies such as Fona/HMW, Codan Insurance, Volvo Trucks and Ensure Insurance Broker, she now inspires to new leadership through her book, "Energetic Leadership", keynotes, facilitation and mentoring for leaders in her company Energetic Leadership – Bronte ApS.

Gitte holds a BSc in Business Administration from Copenhagen Business School and an MBA semester from the University of Victoria. She also has traditional leadership courses and certifications in intuitive and feminine future leadership, inner sustainability, and energy-based leadership. Gitte has lived in London, Sydney, and Kuala Lumpur and currently resides in Denmark.

www.linkedin.com/in/gittemadelaire/
www.energeticleadership.eu

Thank you for buying the book Energetic Leadership –
I hope it brings you true energy in your leadership.

For complementary material, please visit
www.energeticleadership.eu/resources

Sources and glossary

1   HeartMath Institute
2   Net positive employee barometer, 2023, Paul Polman
3   Bruce Lipton, https://www.brucelipton.com/
4   Nature - Fearful memories haunt mouse descendants, 2013, Ewen Gallaway
5   Book Kvantelivet, 2021, Henning Richard Jensen, M.Sc.
6   https://en.wikipedia.org/wiki/Energy
7   https://en.wikipedia.org/wiki/Vacuum
8   Energetic Leadership Model, 2022, copyright Gitte Madelaire
9   https://en.wikipedia.org/wiki/Mindset#Fixed_and_growth_mindset
10   Growth mindset model, 2022, Mette Ploug Meineche, text to illustration
11   Global megatrends from CIFS - Copenhagen Institute for Futures Studies
12   https://ing.dk/holdning/den-4-industrielle-revolution
13   https://en.wikipedia.org/wiki/Fourth_Industrial_Revolution
14   "You Create Your Life - quantum physics explains how" (Originally in Danish: "Derfor skaber
         du dit eget liv - med baggrund i kvantefysikken"), 2021, Henning R. Jensen, M.Sc. https://
         kvantelivet.dk/
15   Seminar DTU Skylab by Kiosk Studio, marts 2022. https://www.skylab.dtu.dk
16   https://overshoot.footprintnetwork.org/about-earth-overshoot-day/
17   Rapport from 2023 by Thalmus Mahand & Cam Caldwell about Quiet Quitting - Causes and
         Opportunities
18   Harvard Business Review, Damron, 2018
19   https://en.wikipedia.org/wiki/Baby_boomers
20   https://en.wikipedia.org/wiki/Generation_X
21   https://pkmedier.dk/
22   https://en.wikipedia.org/wiki/Generation_Z
23   Keynote by Emilia van Hauen, 24.1.2023, Mccrindle Generations, Alpha defined. https://en.wiki-
         pedia.org/wiki/Generation_Alpha
24   www.modernelderacademy.com
25   Human Revolution, Februar 2023, Renate Edsbjerg - www.humanrevolution.dk
26   https://www.theweek.ooo/
27   Reinventing Organizations, Frederic Laloux
28   https://en.wikipedia.org/wiki/Environmental,_social,_and_corporate_governance
29   https://finance.ec.europa.eu/capital-markets-union-and-financial-markets/company-report-
         ing-and-auditing/company-reporting/corporate-sustainability-reporting_en/
30   https://da.wikipedia.org/wiki/Pseudoarbejde
31   https://stephangrabmeier.de/bani-versus-vuca/
32   Workbook by Renata Edsbjerg, 2023, www.humanrevolution.dk
33   https://www.universalfuturist.com/
34   https://www.futurescouts.dk/
35   https://denstoredanske.lex.dk/ego, https://en.wikipedia.org/wiki/Ego
36   https://en.wikipedia.org/wiki/Mind
37   https://en.wikipedia.org/wiki/Soul
38   Howard Gardner, Frames of mind, 1983 and Per Fibaek Laursen's interpretation of The Multiple
         Intelligences, 1997
39   Pauline Skov Poulsen, https://www.powerandpeople.com/
40   Psychoanalysis, 1890´s, Sigmund Freud, https://en.wikipedia.org/wiki/Sigmund_Freud
41   https://www.who.int/activities/improving-the-mental-and-brain-health-of-children-and-adoles-
         cents
42   https://www.kathrinekrake.com
43   Book, Kvantelivet, 2021, Henning R. Jensen, M.Sc.
44   https://cathrineyoga.dk/chakraernes-betydning
45   https://en.wikipedia.org/wiki/Chakra
46   https://maraihan.com/7-chakra/

47   https://www.mindvibrations.com/ancient-solfeggio-scale/
48   https://www.powerandpeople.com/
49   https://www.powerandpeople.com/
50   https://en.wikipedia.org/wiki/Insomnia
51   https://en.wikipedia.org/wiki/Insomnia
52   https://www.sciencedaily.com/releases/2021/06/210608092300.htm
53   https://www.who.int/news-room/fact-sheets/detail/obesity-and-overweight
54   https://foedevarestyrelsen.dk/kost-og-foedevarer/maerkning-og-markedsfoering-af-foedevarer/
        frivillig-foedevareinformation/noeglehulsmaerket
55   https://alkaline-institute.dk/
56   https://en.wikipedia.org/wiki/Alkaline_diet
57   https://en.wikipedia.org/wiki/Ayurveda
58   https://www.stabiltblodsukker.dk/blodsukker-ultimative-guide/
59   https://www.cdc.gov/diabetes/managing/manage-blood-sugar.html
60   https://www.who.int/health-topics/diabetes
61   https://www.eyefulness.com
62   Book Energi, Rikke Hertz, 2021
63   https://en.wikipedia.org/wiki/Depth_psychology
64   Interview, June 2022
65   https://www.kundetyper.dk/
66   https://hbr.org/2015/11/the-new-science-of-customer-emotions
67   https://www.mycustomer.com/customer-experience/engagement/the-20-emotions-that-drive-
        or-destroy-value-in-customer-experience
68   https://en.wikipedia.org/wiki/Catching_the_Big_Fish
69   https://en.wikipedia.org/wiki/Meditation
70   https://www.tm.org/
71   https://www.kathrinekrake.com/
72   Dr. Jeffrey D. Thompson, D.C.,B.F.A. Center for Neuroacoustic Research
73   www.powerandpeople.com
74   www.powerandpeople.com

Energetic
The acknowledgement that energy is the
fundamental force in the sensory world

Leadership
The ability to guide and empower yourself and others

Energetic leadership
Consciously leading oneself and others with
energy and intuition as a starting and focal point

Consciousness
A movement of experiences, movements of energy

Soul
Your true self (your spirit)

Mind
Your thoughts, feelings and beliefs

Spirituality
The quality of being concerned with the human spirit
or soul as opposed to material or physical things